If you have kids and they're grown up, or you think they might grow up, you gotta get this book. This is center-cut wisdom and prime guidance.

—JOHN ORTBERG, senior pastor, Menlo
Church; author, *Eternity Is Now in Session*

If you have adult children (or you are about to), don't miss out on this timely message. It's inspirational, grounded, and immeasurably practical. We can't recommend it enough.

—DRS. LES AND LESLIE PARROTT, authors, *New York Times* bestselling *Saving Your Marriage before It Starts*

Jim Burns lives where you and I do. I love his practical, common-sense but biblical counsel. And he has a sense of humor to help us in the tough spots.

—RUTH GRAHAM, author, *In Every Pew Sits a Broken Heart*

Relating to adult children can be one of life's greatest challenges. For all who are looking for practical help, this book is a must read.

—GARY CHAPMAN, author, *The Five Love Languages*

In his latest book, Jim Burns offers practical, down-to-earth wisdom for the mom or dad who wants to journey through this transition in a healthy, biblically based way.

—JIM DALY, president, Focus on the Family

Jim Burns provides great solutions at several levels: engaging and vulnerable stories, biblical principles, and specific skills. You will change the way you relate to your adult k̲i̲d̲s̲ ̲f̲o̲r̲ ̲t̲h̲e̲ ̲b̲e̲t̲t̲e̲r̲.

—DR. JOHN TOWNSEND,
The Townsend Institute o̲

Jim Burns never ceases to amaze me. Yet another practical, encouraging book that you will turn to repeatedly to help you better love, listen to, and laugh with your young adult children.

Healthy family relationships are the pearls of life; this book will help you not only to discover that but also to recover what may have gotten lost along the way.

This helpful, practical, and at times profoundly insightful book will help you either save or build your relationship with your grown children. You'll be immensely grateful you read it.

DOING LIFE
WITH YOUR
ADULT
CHILDREN

ALSO BY JIM BURNS

Confident Parenting

Creating an Intimate Marriage

10 Building Blocks for a Solid Family

Closer (with Cathy Burns)

Understanding Your Teen

Pass It On

The Purity Code

Teaching Your Children Healthy Sexuality

God Made Your Body (children's book)

How God Makes Babies (children's book)

Getting Ready for Marriage (with Doug Fields)

The First Few Years of Marriage (with Doug Fields)

Faith Conversations for Families

DOING LIFE WITH YOUR ADULT CHILDREN

KEEP YOUR MOUTH SHUT & THE WELCOME MAT OUT

JIM BURNS

ZONDERVAN

Doing Life with Your Adult Children
Copyright © 2019 by Jim Burns

Requests for information should be addressed to:
Zondervan, *3900 Sparks Dr. SE, Grand Rapids, Michigan 49546*

ISBN 978-0-310-35377-5 (softcover)
ISBN 978-0-310-35776-6 (audio)
ISBN 978-0-310-35379-9 (ebook)

Published in association with the literary agency of WordServe Literary Group, Ltd., www.wordserveliterary.com.

Cover design: Brand Navigation
Cover photos: iStock / Shutterstock
Interior design: Denise Froehlich

Printed in the United States of America

19 20 21 22 23 LSC 10 9 8 7 6 5 4 3 2 1

To Randy and Susan Bramel

✦•✦

Thank you for your inspiration and mentorship

in my life. Thank you for your leadership

at HomeWord. Most of all, thank you for

being the "transitional generation" for your

children and your children's children.

CONTENTS

✦•✦

PREFACE

✦•✦

Two key experiences compelled me to write *Doing Life with Your Adult Children*—one at a Christian leadership conference and another in a series of focus groups.

My good friends Dan and Pam Chun, who lead HIM (Hawaiian Island Ministries), asked me to speak on "Parenting Your Adult Child" at their annual leadership conference in Honolulu. I must admit, as much as I love Dan and Pam, I laughed and said, "I have nothing to offer on the subject of parenting an adult child, and frankly, Cathy and I desperately need to *attend* that seminar." But the Chuns refused to take no for an answer, and I finally agreed to develop a seminar for the conference.

I opened my session with these words: "If you are anything like me, being the parent of an adult child is probably much more complicated than you ever imagined. Most of us have adult children—which is a bit of an oxymoron—who have violated our values and chosen a different path than we would have chosen for them." The crowd groaned in pained recognition. I have never had a reaction like that before. It seemed that nearly everyone at the seminar was navigating a complex story and living with mixed feelings about being a parent of an adult child. After the seminar, I knew I'd hit a nerve when I spent two and a half hours listening to one story of difficulty after another.

A few years after the seminar in Honolulu, HomeWord held seven focus groups with parents of adult children. Our goal was to listen to parents and hear their felt needs. In six of the seven focus groups, at least one parent broke down and cried. Although not every participant was brokenhearted, I heard many painful stories of adult children who were violating family values and faith, cohabitating, struggling with addictions, divorcing, experiencing gender confusion, suffering financial complications, or failing to launch. These parents were filled with confusion, shock, and other painful emotions. Some blamed themselves, while others blamed spouses, ex-spouses, or the corrupting influence of contemporary culture. After experiencing the intense emotions and extreme interest of those in the focus groups, I knew my experience in Honolulu had not been a fluke. I needed to write this book.

I have spent the last several years researching this complex topic, listening to parents, and discussing these issues with parents and adult children alike. Cathy and I have lived out the principles on these pages with our own family. My goal has been to write a book that is both hopeful and enlightening, practical and life changing. You'll have to let me know what you think.

THANK YOU

✦•✦

To Cathy, for the amazing example you are to our children—and now to our grandchildren—of consistent faith and abiding love. I know I'm a very blessed man.

To Christy, Rebecca, and Heidi, for allowing us to "experiment" on you with our parenting skills! Even though the learning curve has been steep at times, you have become wonderful adults with whom we love doing life together.

To Randy Bramel, Tom Purcell, Rod Emery, and Terry Hartshorn: I look forward to being with you every Tuesday morning and I have learned so much from your lives.

To Cindy Ward, for more than fourteen years of partnership in ministry, for your tireless work ethic, and for the incredible example you are of a life well lived.

To Greg Johnson, for your friendship and for being a world-class literary agent.

To Sandy Vander Zicht, for your distinguished career in the world of publishing. I am so thankful and honored to have had the opportunity to work with you on this project.

AN INVITATION TO KEEP THE WELCOME MAT OUT

Something wakes me up. I look at the clock and it is 2:30 a.m. I then discover what, or rather *who*, disturbed my sleep. It's my wife, Cathy. She is just lying there next to me with her eyes wide open.

"What's up?" I ask. "You okay?"

"Yes, I'm okay," she says. "I was just thinking about Becca."

"Is she okay?" I ask.

"I guess so," Cathy replies. "I just don't know."

I give her hand a reassuring pat. "Is there anything I can do for you?"

"No," she says, "just go back to sleep."

Most parents I've talked with have told me they lost sleep worrying about their kids when the kids were younger, but I've been surprised to discover how many parents of adult children tell me the same thing. I often hear statements like these:

- "My son's choices are breaking my heart."
- "I feel like I don't know what my role as her parent is anymore."

- "He needs to get a job!"
- "Every time I give my daughter some heartfelt advice, she bites my head off."
- "I'm still in shock that he doesn't go to church anymore."
- "Where did I go wrong?"

Can you relate? If so, know that you are far from alone and that the pages that follow were written with you in mind. Although this book can't magically take away any problem you have with your adult child, I hope it will give you the perspective, insight, and practical guidance you need to move your relationship in a positive direction. We'll tackle some of the toughest and most common issues faced by parents who are struggling with their adult children. And we'll explore nine principles that can help you through these thorny issues in productive ways.

It's important to me that you know these nine principles aren't just abstract theory. They were developed and applied primarily in the lab of doing life with my own adult children. Although my career has given me a platform to write and speak on topics such as parenting, marriage, and relationships, this is a much more personal book. I wanted to figure out how to be the best possible dad to my adult children, who are my deepest joy and greatest challenge. At this stage in my journey there is much more joy than challenge, but it hasn't always been easy.

The issues covered in this book come from our own challenges as parents, as well the challenges of thousands of other parents who have shared their stories with me. As I listened to story after story, I began to see patterns and commonalities. When I went looking for resources, I was surprised to discover that, compared with the literature available for the early years of parenting, there is relatively little available about the challenges of parenting an adult child. Yet we will spend more time as a parent of an adult child than we will as the parent of a young child and adolescent.

As I wrote the book, I kept an old Starbucks cup on my desk. It was a reminder that I wanted these pages to read more like a conversation between two friends talking about their kids than an expert doling out a monolog of advice. Friends tell stories and share dreams. Friends give ideas to each other and confess worries. Friends give each other hope and encouragement. I've often said that "people learn best when *they* talk, not when I talk."

If we were sitting together over coffee, we could have a great conversation. But since we aren't able to sit together, I've created questions for reflection at the end of each chapter. You can use them on your own or discuss them with your spouse or in a small group.[1]

My goal is to give you hope and encouragement on your journey. Like Cathy and me, you may have nights when you lie awake and wonder, *What in the world is going on with my kid?* Today, now that our kids have gotten older, we are experiencing the incredible joy of grandparenting and have made the transition from an adult-child relationship with our kids to our dream of an adult-adult relationship. Has it been easy? For us, not really. Have these principles helped us? Yes, immeasurably.

My prayer is that these pages will reassure you that life with your adult child can be the best years of your relationship.

Keep the welcome mat out.

CHAPTER 1

YOU'RE FIRED!

PRINCIPLE 1: YOUR ROLE AS THE PARENT MUST CHANGE

✦•✦

"Be nice to your adult children. They will most likely be the ones who someday take away your car keys and usher you into the convalescent care facility."

I don't know about you, but as our three daughters became adults, we didn't see all the changes coming. When our kids were in their early twenties, they told us in one way or another that they were now grown up, even though—from our perspective—they weren't always acting like it. They wanted to be treated as adults but were still mostly dependent on our income and were making some lifestyle choices that collided with our values. "I thought life was supposed to be easier and less complicated when our kids became adults," my wife said.

Over the past decade, many people have told me that being the parent of an adult child was not what they expected. One woman quoted a line from the movie *Hitch*, in which the lead character says after a disastrous dating experience, "I saw that going differently in my mind." What parent of an adult child hasn't said something like that? Some kids who now live in adult bodies still act a bit like children. Or at least their parents think so.

Here is the good news: most adult children eventually do become responsible and independent. They may zigzag through their younger adult years, taking a few steps forward and a few steps back, and there might be a U-turn or some false starts along the way, but it eventually happens. The challenge is that becoming an adult seems to be taking longer for this generation than it has for any previous generation. And that slower transition isn't easy for the parent or the adult child.

Although you and your child are traveling different paths, you're on a parallel journey of reinventing your relationship. It's better when you navigate it together, but neither of you have passed this way before, and even if you have made the transition with one child, the next child likely will approach the transition to adulthood differently. You might find yourself with some degree of day-to-day parenting duty that stretches past the eighteen-year mark—or even the twenty-five- to thirty-year mark, especially if your adult children move back home for some reason. You no doubt will experience bewilderment when your grown kids violate your values or live differently from how they were raised, but your goal must remain the same: to help your children transition to responsible adulthood. To do that, you need to first understand your old job description as a parent and then create a new one.

YOUR OLD JOB DESCRIPTION

When our kids were young, my wife, Cathy, and I felt fairly comfortable in our parenting roles. It wasn't always easy and there were some bumps in the road, but for the first two decades we were clear about our jobs. We were in control and it was our clear-cut responsibility to be our children's providers, caretakers, and nurturers. Even if our kids disagreed, they knew that ultimately we were the bosses.

Then adulthood abruptly showed up, and we weren't ready

for it. For us, it happened on the day each kid went away to college. Now they were setting their own hours, making travel decisions we didn't always agree with, and spending money on things and experiences we would not have approved of just a few months before. To them, church attendance was now an option rather than a commitment. Cathy and I realized we were losing a part of our parenting job description that we liked, which was the control. In a very short amount of time, we moved from having daily input in our kids' lives and doing hands-on parenting, to more of an intermittent and distant kind of parenting. Most transitions aren't easy, and we found the transition from our old job description to be especially challenging.

It's important to acknowledge your old job description as a parent so that you can set it aside. That's the only way to make room for your new job description. It's also important to know that this transition of moving from daily involvement and hands-on parenting to a more intermittent involvement will likely be an easier move for your kids than it is for you. Expect to have a transition period within your transition. In our case, we thought of it as a unique and somewhat awkward dance in which neither we nor our kids knew the right moves. There was plenty of stepping on toes and renegotiating boundaries until we found our rhythm with each other. And just when we thought we were dancing well with one child, the next child went to college and we had to do the awkward dance all over again.

YOUR NEW JOB DESCRIPTION

Since all children are different, there is no template for a new job description for parenting adult children. You may have to redefine your role differently for each of your kids. But before you can create that new job description, or better yet a new kind of relationship with your adult children, there is one important thing you need to do. You must love them enough to let them go. Rewriting the script and establishing a new adult-to-adult relationship with your kids requires firing yourself from your old job of day-to-day nurturing and being "in control" of your kids, and embracing a new role that is not as daily or as hands-on as before. Hard as it is, the role you play in your children's lives must diminish in order for them to transition from adolescence to responsible adulthood.

If you are in or have already been through this transitional stage, you know that it's complicated, often messy, and can sometimes feel like you're walking on eggshells. One dad I know described it this way: "My son and I had been very close, even in the teen years," he said. "As he approached adulthood, I kept doing what I had always been doing, but my son reacted

---

A Prayer of Relinquishment

God, I relinquish my children to your care and watchfulness. Give me the courage to let go as they move—sometimes ever so slowly—toward responsible adulthood. Grant me discernment to know when to carefully intervene, and the restraint to do so only when absolutely necessary. I acknowledge that this is one of the hardest transitions I have ever had to make, and that I need your guidance and insight. In all things, help me to love my children as you love them—lavishly and with grace. Amen.

---

in strange ways. Most of the time, he didn't want my advice. I'm a pastor, and frankly, I give good advice. Regardless, he moved away from my control but still wanted my influence—on his terms. It took a few years and some bumps and ego bruises along the way to figure out what this new adult-to-adult relationship would look like." He went on to say, "Sometimes we still experience bumps in our relationship, especially when he is making decisions I'm not happy about. But I've had to realize that his vision for his life is different from my vision for his life. One of the most difficult things I had to do was relinquish my adult child to God and release my control over him." My friend eloquently described the idea of reinventing the relationship to help his son become a responsible adult.

Although there are no formulas or job description templates for making the transition to an adult-to-adult relationship with your child, Cathy and I discovered some meaningful strategies to help you along the way. We called these our guiding principles and needed to refer to them often, especially at the beginning of the transition. The quicker you can embrace your new role and, yes, even grieve the loss of your old role, the better it is for everyone. Here are four strategies to help you embrace your new job description.

1. Be encouraging but not intrusive. You are a consultant at their will. Your job is to be caring and supportive of your child, to mentor only when called upon, and to be your child's biggest cheerleader. Don't be like the mother who told her daughter, "Honey, put on your coat. It's cold outside!" Her daughter, who was vice president of a successful tech firm, shot back, "Mom, I'm forty-five years old and I can decide for myself when I put a coat on!" Her mother simply added, "I'm still your mother and you need to listen to me." As well-meaning as the mom may have been, her daughter considered her intrusive.

Being intrusive means inserting yourself into your child's life in ways that are uninvited or unwelcome. Not being intrusive means promoting your child to full adult status and developing a new adult-to-adult relationship, while at the same time being encouraging and supportive. One of the ways Cathy and I learned to be encouraging was to hold our tongues and not say everything we thought. Instead of giving voice to whatever we disagreed with, we focused on cheering whatever we could affirm.

My friend Rob summarizes his approach to being encouraging rather than intrusive this way: "Earn the right to be heard." Rob was concerned about his daughter Angela's lifestyle choices. In one encounter, he pulled out a "dad list" of concerns and went through them one by one. Needless to say, it did not go over very well with his daughter. The result was tears and anger. The more he expressed his disapproval, the farther away Angela moved from what had once been a close relationship. So Rob changed his approach. One day he called her up and said, "How would you like to go snowboarding together for a couple of days?" Angela loved to snowboard and Rob thought she would jump at the chance, but she hesitated before accepting the invitation. It was clear she didn't want a repeat of their conversation.

The day before Rob arrived to pick up his daughter, he was tempted to write up another list of concerns he wanted to discuss. He decided instead to put all of his energy into simply enjoying and encouraging his daughter. Even though he still had concerns, he also had strong reasons to affirm her. Rob and Angela had a wonderful weekend together, laughing, sharing, and eating good food. Even so, as Rob drove home after dropping her off, he wondered whether he'd done the right thing by not talking with her about his concerns.

Rob didn't have to wonder for long. Just as he pulled into his driveway, he got this text from Angela: "Dad, that was one of the best times I've ever had with you! Thank you so much for snowboarding and the great meals. I love you so much. Oh, also, I know you probably had your 'dad list' with you, and I wanted to give you a quick update." Angela went on to tell her dad that she was making some changes in many of the areas in which he had concerns. Today, she is happily married and still very close to her dad, who has become a mentor to her. He chose to be encouraging and not intrusive, and the results were twofold: he earned the right to be heard, and he developed a more positive and trusting relationship with his daughter.

Being encouraging rather than intrusive is one of those disciplines in which you might find yourself taking four steps forward and then a step or two backward. In our hearts we know encouragement is much more effective than intrusion, but it's not always easy to do. So go easy on yourself if you fall back into old habits, but practice the discipline of encouragement. You'll get a much more positive response with affirmation than with meddling.

2. Be caring, but do not enable dependency. There is a difference between caring and enabling dependency. Clearly, your new role involves loving care, but it can't be a form of care that keeps your child dependent on you. Some parents keep tight reins on their adult children because they are unknowingly struggling with their need to be needed. Their motives may be admirable, but caring that enables dependency isn't healthy.

Take John and Sylvia, for example. They took money out of their retirement savings to loan their son and his new wife the money to buy a very nice home. That may seem like a loving thing to do, but John and Sylvia didn't have the money to spare. Now they are suffering through some rough financial situations while their son and daughter-in-law enjoy a home that neither they nor their kids can afford. They are helping to make monthly payments to keep the kids from losing the house. John and Sylvia viewed their loan as caring for their son and daughter-in-law, but the truth is that they were enabling dependency. If they had it to do over again, they would not have used their retirement savings to buy their kids a dream house they couldn't afford on their own. It's a classic example of a generous act that backfired. It's what happens when we confuse caring with enabling dependency.

So what else might John and Sylvia have done? They could have allowed their kids to learn delayed gratification by saying no to the down payment. Or agreed to help out with a down payment on a more modest home the kids could afford on their income. The best decision is always one that does not enable dependence.

Your job as a parent is to prepare your kids for adult life and then let them go. You are still their parent and that will never change, but the relationship must transition from dependency into a place of greater empowerment and maturity for your child. Independence is the goal. This means your adult children take full responsibility for their finances, actions, relationships, and growth and development.

3. Invest in your emotional, physical, and spiritual health. Brenda and her husband, Ted, sat in my office brokenhearted.

Their daughter Lindsay had just moved in with her boyfriend. She had also confessed to something they had long suspected, which was her use of illicit drugs.

"What did we do wrong?" Brenda asked. "It seems like everyone else's adult kids are making better decisions than ours."

"Maybe we should have made Lindsay go on more mission trips," Ted said.

"Every year at Christmas when we saw the picture-perfect families in cards and on social media," Brenda lamented, "we had the same thought: 'What is wrong with our parenting skills?'"

Although they couldn't name it, Brenda and Ted were experiencing shame. As our conversation continued, we considered how to deal with Lindsay's problems, but I also asked them about a problem I wasn't sure they knew they had.

"Lindsay's actions must be devastating to you," I said. "It sounds like you are really depleted." Ted nodded and Brenda's eyes filled with tears.

"What are you doing to maintain your emotional, physical, relational, and even spiritual health?" At this, Ted's eyes welled up with tears and Brenda began to sob. Ted put his arm around his wife and said simply, "We aren't doing anything for us. And it's killing us."

My heart went out to them because I knew the pain of a troubled child was depleting them in so many ways. My counsel wasn't anything new, but it seemed to help them.

"I'm sure you've heard what a flight attendant says when you get on an airplane, right? If there is a need for oxygen, put on your own oxygen mask first and then help your child." The looks on their faces told me that they understood.

You won't be of any benefit to your child if you are gasping for air. Working on your emotional, physical, and spiritual health not only helps you to be stronger for your child but also helps you to gain a clearer perspective on any shame or regret you may be feeling.

When kids make poor or disappointing decisions, many parents experience the silent shame Brenda described. A friend of mine once said to me, "When your children are young, they climb all over you and step on your feet. When they are older and make poor choices, they step all over your heart." Of course, not all adult children break their parents' hearts, but the transition is still difficult for most and usually involves a great deal of loss. Author Judith Viorst is right when she says, "Letting our children go, and letting our dreams for our children go, must be counted among our necessary losses."[2]

Whenever we experience a loss, we need to grieve it. If we don't grieve the relationship we once had with our children, we won't be able to embrace the new relationship we want to have with them. When our children no longer need us the way they once did, that's a loss. I'm reminded of this every time I watch my grandson, James. I love how his mommy and daddy are the center of his universe—he needs them for everything. But it's also a bittersweet experience when I realize that I was once the center of my children's universe, and now I'm not. For my children to be healthy and independent, I had to release them and grieve the loss.

Being willing to put yourself in the back seat of your children's lives—and to grieve the loss of the front seat—is what gives you the chance to change the relationship and make it wonderfully different. But that won't happen if you aren't emotionally, physically, and spiritually healthy yourself. That's why you must invest in self-care as your role with your adult kids changes. A friend of mine puts it this way: "Untended fires soon become nothing but a pile of ashes." If you put all of your energy into caring for your adult kids, you'll only end up depleted. "Self-care is not selfish," writes my mentor, Gary Smalley. It is perhaps the best thing you can do for yourself and for your family.

Self-care means being proactive in caring for your mind, body, and soul. That might include spending time with people you enjoy, engaging in activities that replenish you, being physically active, or even trying something new and exciting. If you have an adult child who is struggling, you will also want to surround yourself with a team of people who can be your support. Take it from Moses.

Remember the story in the Bible when the Israelites were battling the Amalekites? When Moses held up his hands, the Israelites advanced against the Amalekites, but when he grew weary and could no longer hold up his hands, the Amalekites advanced against the Israelites. So Aaron and Hur found a stone for Moses to sit on and each man held up one of Moses' hands. With their help, Moses' hands remained steady throughout the long battle, and the Israelites won a great victory against the Amalekites. As you navigate the losses and challenges of transitioning your relationship with your adult children, make sure you have a team around you to share your burdens.

4. Have serious fun. Transitioning to a new role isn't all loss and tears. There is also some serious fun to be had! You can't determine the outcome of your children's lives, so shift your focus to creating fun and enjoyable experiences you can share.

"A cheerful heart is good medicine," wrote wise King Solomon, "but a broken spirit saps a person's strength" (Prov. 17:22 NLT). Your attitude toward your adult children will go a long way toward determining your relationship with them. Families that laugh and develop happy traditions draw closer to each other over time. One of the principles Cathy and I have relied on is this: "Words don't always lead to connection, but enjoyable connections lead to words." What are the activities and experiences your adult children enjoy? Chances are good that engaging in those activities with them will enhance your relationship. For many adult children, the fun factor is what determines their desire to relate to their parents on a deeper level.

When I was in grad school, I studied traits of healthy families and later wrote a book on the subject.[3] One of the top ten traits is play. Come to find out, families who play together really do stay together. Play, fun, laughter, and the creation of lifelong memories are essential for keeping your relationship with your adult kids strong. Play is a "love currency" that makes a deposit into your children's lives no matter what their age. Having fun together also can open a closed heart (as it did with Rob's daughter Angela), reduce stress, and even help heal broken relationships.

How is the fun factor in your family? One of the great benefits of moving from a parent-child relationship to an adult-adult relationship is that you can begin a deeper friendship with your adult child. One of the strongest elements of friendship is having fun together. If you want to transition well, make initiating fun part of your new job description. And keep in mind that fun doesn't have to be expensive. It might be sharing enjoyable meals, playing golf, window shopping, or anything your family enjoys doing. What are the fun experiences that will draw your relationship closer?

Embracing these four strategies for adopting a new job description can turn a tough transition into a meaningful transition. Too often we focus on how to manage our kids' transition to adulthood when the best way to facilitate their transition might be to change our job description. No one said it would be easy or that there wouldn't be bumps along the way, but changing your job description is a great way to start. The result is that your legacy continues to the next generation.

LEAVING AN IMPACTFUL LEGACY

During a time of tension or deep disappointment, it can be difficult to think about creating a positive legacy for your children, but don't give in to despair or minimize your power to create a positive climate of influence and leave a legacy in your children's lives. Your attitude, lifestyle, values, faith, and example impact your kids in ways you may never fully know. Author and pastor Chuck Swindoll summarized building legacy so well when he said, "Each day of our lives we make deposits in the memory banks of our children." I know that was certainly the case with my parents.

My father had his flaws, but he was a good man and I looked up to him. At the end of his life, he was quite feeble, and he fell and broke his hip while using his walker. The doctor told us he thought he could fix the hip, but he was concerned that if Dad didn't get up and move around after the surgery, he would die of pneumonia. Two weeks later, after a successful hip surgery, he was indeed placed in hospice care because he hadn't gotten up and moved around. He eventually died exactly as the doctor forewarned—from pneumonia.

I was alone with my dad in his room at a convalescent hospital a few days before his death when an energetic physical therapist came into the room and asked my dad to get up because it was time for physical therapy. I thought that a bit strange given my dad's condition but decided to watch what would happen. Dad gave it a valiant try, but he almost fell out of bed in the process. I jumped up and caught him. The physical therapist seemed surprised at his frailty and then noticed she had the wrong chart!

"Bob, how did you break your hip?" the therapist asked.

"It was a motorcycle accident," Dad said without missing a beat. I smiled. The therapist looked at me with a puzzled expression.

"Actually," I said, "he fell from his walker, but he did have a motorcycle accident about forty-five years ago."

She smiled, looked back and forth between Dad and me, and then said, "Bob, this guy looks like he is your son. Do you have any other children?"

"Yes," Dad said, "his mom and I have four boys." He listed our names. He then added, "And I'm proud of all my boys." It brought tears to my eyes to hear Dad say that about us. "I'm looking forward to being with God soon in heaven," he added.

The therapist didn't quite know how to respond to that. She smiled again.

"I've lived a good life and I really have no regrets," Dad said. "God is waiting for me in eternity." At this point, tears again welled up in my eyes, and when I looked at the physical therapist, I saw she also had tears in her eyes. She lovingly put her hand on my father's shoulder and said, "Goodbye, Bob. You are a good, good man. Thank you."

Later, as I reflected on what my dad had said, I was reminded of the studies psychiatrist Elisabeth Kübler-Ross had done on death and dying. As a researcher, Dr. Kübler-Ross spent many years interviewing people who were near death. One of her findings was that at the end of life, most people think primarily about two things: a right relationship with God, and a right relationship with those they love.

This was certainly the case with my dad. In his final days on earth, he was at peace, and that taught me a valuable lesson: there is absolutely nothing more important in life than a right relationship with God and a right relationship with family. Ultimately, that's what defines the legacy you leave your children. As difficult as it is to raise children and then maintain that bond through the complexity of relating to them as adults, what matters most isn't the material legacy you leave behind but the legacy of love and faith you hand down to the next generation.

When our kids are younger, most of us are so busy with the demands of day-to-day parenting that it's hard to focus on leaving a legacy. But as your role and job description change, you can focus on what is most important, which is leaving your child a legacy of love.

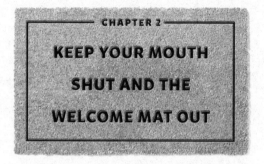

CHAPTER 2

KEEP YOUR MOUTH SHUT AND THE WELCOME MAT OUT

PRINCIPLE 2: UNSOLICITED ADVICE IS USUALLY TAKEN AS CRITICISM

➤•➤

"But why does she need to go to Europe to find herself when I have all the answers for her life right here?"

‡·‡·‡

I know there is a time to speak up and a time to keep my mouth shut," said a friend of mine. "I just haven't figured out what to do when." Maybe you can relate. Knowing what to say and what not to say is one of the major challenges most of us face in transitioning to an adult relationship with a son or daughter. Although there are exceptions, I've learned that in most cases the best policy for parents is to bite their tongues and remain silent. Withholding advice goes against our nature as parents, but unsolicited advice is usually taken as criticism.

Many parents of adult children tell me that the most difficult part of their new job description is abstaining from giving advice when they know they're correct. For more than two decades, our reflex was to offer our guidance. It's hardwired into every parent's DNA. We have advice to offer for everything from potty training to first dates and more. So it is sometimes a shock when we discover that our kids not only view our advice as criticism but also aren't asking for it.

Here are four important guidelines to help you keep your relationship strong and avoid the trap of giving unsolicited advice.

1. TRUST THAT EXPERIENCE IS A
BETTER TEACHER THAN ADVICE

However much a parent views giving advice as an act of love, most adult children resent it. They strive for independence and view a parent's giving advice as telling them what to do or restricting their freedom. If you choose to give them advice rather than encourage their independence, they will run from you. When it comes to giving advice, author Jane Isay writes, "Don't give it. They don't like it. They don't want it. They resent it."[4]

Instead of steering your children in the way you think they should go, trust that experience is a much better teacher. When you give them the independence and respect they desire, they'll learn from their experiences of victory and defeat. If we keep our mouths shut and keep the welcome mat out, we increase the odds that our children will come to us for guidance on their own. If we choose to continue giving them unwanted advice, even if it's great advice with the best of intentions, our intrusive counsel will ultimately hurt the relationship. Some call that the "high cost of good advice."

One of my wife Cathy's love languages is "giving advice." Whenever she runs across an article she thinks might benefit someone in the family, she cuts it out of the magazine or forwards the web link. She is our go-to authority on everything from healthy lifestyle issues to spiritual growth and numerous other aspects of life. And she not only gives good advice but also lives out what she advises the rest of us to do.

One day when our kids were younger, we were on vacation in a small town in England when we came upon a sign in a doorway that read "Citizen's Advice Counsel." The kids shouted, "Mom, this is the perfect job for you!" Her husband (that would be me) was smart enough to keep his mouth shut. Cathy just laughed and said, "You're probably right." For a person like Cathy, to whom advice-giving comes naturally, it's especially difficult to bite her tongue and keep good advice to herself. But she has learned the wisdom of not saying everything she thinks. When she does that, it's amazing how many times our children end up seeking her counsel.

Here is the scriptural principle: "Everyone should be quick to listen, slow to speak and slow to become angry" (James 1:19). That's especially important for those of us who are fix-it people. If I am a fix-it person and my kids have a problem, I consider it my job to intervene. That's what I do, and that's who I am—Mr. Fix-It. But unless our adult kids ask us for help, we must resist the impulse to fix their problems.

When you're tempted to give unsolicited advice, pause and ask yourself this question: Does it really matter? Most issues don't really matter as much as we think they do. I love this bit of wisdom from Winston Churchill: "You will never reach your destination if you stop and throw stones at every dog that barks." Keep your eyes on the destination, which is a healthy and loving relationship with your adult children. Don't get distracted by the things that don't really matter. Adult children don't distinguish between what we consider an innocent remark or desire to fix a problem, and parental control. If we want to keep the welcome mat out, we need to keep our mouths shut.

2. GIVE RESPECT: NO ADULT WANTS TO BE TOLD WHAT TO DO

My daughter Christy is a capable young adult, an incredible mother of two, and happily married. Not long ago, she was telling me about a challenge she was facing, and I said, "Christy, do you mind if I give you some advice on that situation?" Her answer surprised me.

"Not right now, Dad," she said. "Maybe later."

Are you kidding me? I thought. *People actually pay me to give advice, and furthermore, I have some really good counsel that you need.* But it was clear that my advice was not what she wanted at that moment. I needed to respect that in the same way I would respect it in any other adult who chose not to hear something I had to share.

Now that your child is an adult, decisions need to be in his or her hands, not yours. This is true whether or not your grownup is acting like a grownup. One of the greatest gifts you can give your children is to respect them as adults. If you don't give them respect, it's pretty much guaranteed they will close the door on your guidance. Don't be like the mom who had the following exchange with her grown son, who'd moved back home after his divorce.

"You need to be home by 9:00 p.m. or I won't be able to cook you a warm dinner."

"Mom, sometimes I work late," he responded, "and I'm very capable of getting my own meal on those nights."

"Then you need to tell your boss you won't work late," she shot back.

"Why?" he asked.

"Because I'm your mother and you need to obey me," she said.

I have a feeling that mother hadn't revised her parental job description since the time her boy was in middle school. Here's the point: when you are intrusive and give unsolicited guidance, your kids don't hear it and they view it as a sign of disrespect.

I've found that so much of the way we give respect to our kids is in the tone of our conversations. By tone, I mean our voice, our demeanor, and even the atmosphere we bring to the conversation. We also need to be clear about the difference between having a conversation and giving a lecture. A conversation conveys respect; a lecture doesn't.

I remember a serious conversation I had with one of my daughters about lifestyle choices when she was in college. I was sad and frustrated that she had made some choices that were not moving her forward. Apparently, my tone wasn't very good, because she later said, "You didn't say you were disappointed in me, but I know you were totally disappointed in me." I did not mean to convey "total" disappointment in her, because it wasn't an all or nothing situation, but that's what my tone conveyed. Author and pastor Ronald Greer writes, "Whenever we are intrusive, what they hear is not the lesson we are trying to share but the message that we don't really respect that they are now grown."[5] Tone is important, and some of us can be tone deaf. But when we offer advice with the respect we would give any other adult, we open the door to a healthy adult-to-adult relationship.

3. YOU ARE NOW A MENTOR AND A COACH

If you want your adult kids to listen to you, you need to transition from being a controlling parent to being a mentor and coach. You do this in part by becoming your children's biggest supporter. Everyone needs affirmation and encouragement,

**How to Tell the Difference between
a Conversation and a Lecture**

You know you are giving a lecture when:
- You do most of the talking
- Your voice is raised
- You sound a little preachy
- You sound like you are speaking to a child
- Your statements make you sound superior

You know you are having a conversation when:
- You are listening to and reflecting on what the other person says
- You engage in a dialog
- Your tone and demeanor show respect
- Your language is free from "you should" statements
- You have been given permission to speak into the other person's life

including your adult children. Remember the line in the movie *Field of Dreams*? "If you build it, they will come." The movie line, of course, refers to building a baseball field in the middle of an Iowa cornfield. But the same principle applies to your relationship with your children. If you build a relationship of positivity and respect, cheer on your adult children, and then wait, they will seek your advice.

Mentors never push their way toward influence in someone's life; they are invited in. Waiting to be invited into your adult children's lives takes a lot of patience, grace, and understanding, especially if they aren't making great decisions. But I've learned the hard way that conversations with my adult children simply do not go well if I force my agenda on them. I have to wait until they want my influence. Such conversations must be on their timeline, not mine. They need to know I am available, but that's as far as I can go until they ask for more.

When I was in graduate school in Princeton, New Jersey, I was also the area director of Mid-Jersey Young Life. Young Life is a wonderful organization that reaches out to kids, mainly in high school and middle school. One of the best phrases in the Young Life philosophy of youth outreach is "earn the right to be heard." While it may feel like your years of raising your children should automatically give you the right to be heard, it just doesn't work that way. So as you navigate this new phase of your relationship, be patient. Waiting for them to come to you will earn you their trust and, yes, the right to be heard by your grown kids.

4. YOUR WORDS HAVE THE POWER TO BLESS AND TO CURSE

The words you speak to your kids have great power—for good and for not so good. The apostle James puts it this way: "And so blessing and cursing come pouring out of the same mouth" (James 3:10 NLT). I got a vivid reminder of this truth not too long ago when I was talking with a man in his fifties whose life had been tragically marked by angry words his father had said to him when he was just a child. "You will never amount to anything!" his father said. "You will probably end up a worthless drunk like your grandfather." Ouch.

"Did your father ever apologize for those words?" I asked.

"No," he replied. As we talked more about his father, it became clear that his dad hadn't always been abusive, but these words had deeply wounded his heart and mind. The father's words were a curse that became a self-fulfilling prophecy. This man struggled for many years with alcoholism before experiencing a deep conversion to Christ and becoming sober.

The lesson for any parent is to be quick to apologize. There isn't a parent alive who hasn't at one time or another said words they regretted to their child. Imagine the difference it might have made if that man's father had come to him and said, "I didn't mean what I said. I spoke in anger and I apologize for those untrue words." Just a sentence or two with a sincere apology might have changed the trajectory of this man's life. We can never underestimate the power of an apology to bless and heal a relationship.

Virtually every child, young or old, is open to receiving words of blessing. A blessing might take the form of encouragement. With adult children, one of the best phrases to use is, "I believe in you." You can also express your encouragement with statements such as, "You have what it takes to make this business happen," and, "I know you will choose the right kind of relationship." I have a sign in my office that says, "Every child needs at least one significant adult who is irrationally positive about them." It's my prayer that every parent will try to be that person in their child's life.

Over the years, it has been my experience that many of the avoidable problems we have with our adult kids arise from poor communication. That's the bad news. The good news is that healthy communication is a learned skill. This means that even though building a healthy relationship is hard work, we can always learn to be more effective communicators, and so can our kids. Here are three principles of healthy communication you can use to bless your adult children.

1. Ask open-ended questions. Open-ended questions have no agenda and no right answer. They can be asked in a non-judgmental way and are conducive to dialog. Open-ended questions keep us from telling our kids what to do. If I ask, "Don't you think this is the best job for you?" I'm not really asking a question; I'm simply giving my opinion in the guise of a question. An open-ended question is a question to which I do not know the answer. It might be something like, "Which job opportunity seems most aligned with your career goals?" Instead of giving your opinion in disguise, you're giving your child a way to consider options and perhaps to dialog with you as he or she looks for an answer.

2. Talk **with** *them, not* **at** *them.* There is a fine line between talking *at* your child and *with* your child. The simplest way I've found to make sure I'm talking with rather than at is to consider how I talk with my friends. I'm not going to tell my friends what they should do. That's talking at them. Rather, I'm going to create a dialog and work hard at listening. A good friend of mine was working on this principle and told me, "I had to realize that I was still living with the old habit of treating my adult son like he was a child. I was lecturing a married man with two children who also happens to be the vice president of a startup tech firm that has already made him a millionaire." My friend was just figuring out that his son didn't need his dad to talk at him. He was more than capable of figuring things out on his own. What my friend needed to focus on instead was building an adult-to-adult relationship with his son.

3. Speak words of grace. When in doubt, shower your child with grace. The word grace means "unmerited favor." You speak words of grace when you leave loving messages (without advice) on voicemail, when you text positive statements, when you cheer them on, when you refuse to say, "I told you so." When our children experience our grace—especially when something goes wrong in their lives—our unmerited favor reflects the grace of God.

One of the most beautiful stories I've heard about the power of a parent's words was shared with me by Ruth "Bunny" Graham, daughter of the late Billy Graham. Ruth told me a remarkable story of brokenness from her own life and how it made all the difference when her father and mother offered grace instead of unsolicited advice.[6] She had been married for more than eighteen years when she discovered that her husband, who worked for the Billy Graham organization and with whom she had three children, was living a secret life of infidelity. She was devastated and, by her own admission, felt suicidal.

Just a few months after her divorce, and against her parents' counsel, she remarried "on the rebound" but knew within twenty-four hours that she had made a terrible mistake. Her life was in shambles. She packed her belongings, fled her abusive marriage, and started driving. She told me she really didn't know where to go. Finally, she decided to swallow her pride and go home to her parents' house. Yes, her parents had cautioned her about marrying this guy, but for Ruth, home was still the safest refuge she could seek.

As she got closer to her parents' home, she felt nervous and filled with shame. *What are my parents going to say to me?* Even as she rounded the last turn to their home in Montreat,

North Carolina, she wondered how they would greet her. For security reasons, the Graham home had gates that needed to be opened, so she called ahead to alert her parents that she was approaching the house. As the gates opened, the first thing she saw was her father, Billy Graham, pacing the driveway, waiting for her. As she stepped out of the car, he gave her a bear hug and simply said, "Welcome home, Bunny." That was it. No lecture, no superior looks, no condemnation. Just grace, love, and welcome. She told me that she kept waiting for an "I told you so," but it never came. Instead, she received nothing but the open hearts and listening ears of her parents. Ruth's parents helped bring her to a healing place not by what they said but by what they didn't say.

I'm guessing most parents of adult children don't realize that the path toward a vibrant adult-to-adult relationship with their kids has so much to do with biting their tongues. Yet this principle of holding back on advice because it's taken as criticism seems to be one of the most important and effective ways of moving the relationship forward. Will there be slipups? You bet. But over time, the discipline of lovingly keeping our mouths shut can make the difference between having a close-knit relationship and one that is struggling. My motto is, "When in doubt, remain silent." I have the scars on my tongue to prove it.

CHAPTER 3

WHY IS IT TAKING MY KID SO LONG TO GROW UP?

PRINCIPLE 3: YOU CAN'T IGNORE YOUR CHILD'S CULTURE

✦•✦

"Lord, teach me to parent the children I have, not the kids I thought I would have."

‡·‡·‡

Cathy and I met at college freshman orientation and married one week after Cathy graduated. We went on a ten-day honeymoon and then started working. We attended grad school and navigated job changes, but we essentially did the same as many of our friends and moved from college directly into being fully independent adults. Today, that pattern is no longer the norm. Instead, many parents are asking, "When will my grownup kid actually grow up?"

As I mentioned in a previous chapter, many young adults today are in no hurry to grow up. Their motto may be, "Yes, but not yet!" Instead of following a direct path to adulthood, they are meandering toward responsibility and some of life's most significant decisions, such as marrying and having children. For many young adults, finishing college takes longer and is costlier than it was for their parents. Then the graduate wants an adventure, a reward for all the years of hard work college required and a respite before taking a full-time job. They might move in with a love interest, then boomerang home, try several different jobs, and have plenty of experiences to find themselves. It isn't until they approach thirty or even older that they begin to get more serious about settling down to what their parents consider responsible adulthood. Although they delay accepting traditional adult responsibilities, they still want to be treated as adults. While there have always been differences between generations, many authorities today tell us the differences and worldview of this generation are more pronounced than those of previous generations. To be an effective parent in this ever-changing relationship with our kids, we must become students of their culture and mindset.

WHO ARE THESE EMERGING ADULTS?

Each generation develops a mindset and patterns that are unique to it. Here's a simple example from my family that illustrates just one way this plays out across generations. My father and mother were the first to bring a television to their little town in Kansas. It was in their generation that the delivery mechanism for entertainment and news shifted from radio to television. My wife and I were part of the hippy generation known for free love, opposition to the Vietnam War, and flower children. We grew up listening to the Beatles, the Rolling Stones, and the Beach Boys on a record player. Our kids' generation has no need of televisions or record players because they can access their news and entertainment online. In their wired world, white earbuds are practically necessary for life! This is just a simple example, but it demonstrates significant shifts not only in technology but also from one generational culture to the next. If we want to understand our emerging adults, we can't ignore how they are influenced and shaped by their cultural norms.

Each generation produces a cultural shift, some more impactful than others, but this generation of young adults has undeniably brought on such a significant shift in the cultural mindset that it's challenging for those of us in previous generations to understand. Their perspectives, priorities, attitudes, goals, and objectives, as well as lifestyle choices, are markedly different from the ones we grew up with. Here are some of their defining characteristics.

They are shaped by technology. On average, young adults are on a mobile device more than a third of their waking hours per day, leading some to call them "screenagers." They view their device not primarily as a phone but rather as a pocket computer that connects them to the world. If you are going to communicate with your emerging adults, you'd better become tech savvy. When they want to learn something, their best friends are Siri, Alexa, and Google. At HomeWord, when we asked young parents where they get their parenting information, nearly everyone said the internet.

They expect everyone to get a blue ribbon. This is the generation that grew up being affirmed as much for participation as for achievement. Whether they won or lost the game, came in first or last, they received a ribbon or a trophy just for showing up. Although such affirmation started out as an effort to bolster poor self-esteem, it ended up contributing to an entitlement mindset—an expectation of reward regardless of effort or performance. Instead of having poor self-esteem, this generation tends to have an inflated view of themselves. As they enter adulthood, this plays out in several areas, including the belief that they deserve higher pay and more recognition at work. Because they didn't make the connection between effort and reward or grapple with the agony of defeat as children, this generation has trouble accepting the fact that in adult life and work, they don't always get a ribbon or a trophy just for showing up.

They don't live to work, they work to live. Their grandparents had a work ethic that often got in the way of relationships—they lived to work. They worked hard and were loyal to their employers. Today's emerging adult is far less likely to commit to one employer and most likely will have multiple careers. They are part of a generation in which neither employers nor employees expect long-term loyalty. They like to work in teams, although they feel comfortable telecommuting or working outside the office. And fewer emerging adults want to work a typical nine-to-five job, aspiring instead to greater work-life balance than that of previous generations. They are determined not to let work dominate their lives.

They want a healthy marriage and family. No doubt every generation wants a healthy marriage and family, but emerging adults are even more intentional about it once they do get married and start having children. This comes as a surprise to many culture experts because of their slower approach to settling down.

They consider tolerance an essential trait of a loving person. They often consider it unloving to express any kind of disapproval of another person's religion, sexuality, and lifestyle. But this generation tends not to have the same level of tolerance for opposing political views and can be quite vocal about expressing their disagreement or their disapproval. This can cause some strong disagreements around the holiday dinner table.

Many emerging adults have a post-Christian worldview, which means that they no longer see the world through Christian values. This is one of the reasons disagreeing with or disapproving of someone else's lifestyle—even if it conflicts with biblical principles—is considered unloving.

They prioritize adventure seeking. This emerging adult generation values adventure. They travel to exotic places, jump out of airplanes, do extreme sports, and even make adventurous decisions about where they will live. When our youngest daughter, Heidi, and her husband, Matt, let us know that they were moving from the West Coast to the East Coast for nine months, we asked what was prompting the move. "We've always wanted to experience the East Coast," Heidi said, "and we thought it was a good idea to do it before we had kids." At first, we had all the worries any parent would have about job security and cost factors. But the more they explained it, the better it sounded. Cathy started calling it "The Millennial Adventure." No doubt your adult children are more adventuresome than previous generations as well.

You might recognize your adult child in some of these characteristics, but did you know that this stage of life is a fairly recent development? It was psychology professor Jeffrey Arnett who first coined the phrase "emerging adulthood" to describe the years between late adolescence and early adulthood. There were traditionally believed to be four stages of life: childhood, adolescence, adulthood, and old age. Today, we have infancy, childhood, adolescence, emerging adulthood, adulthood, and senior adulthood. In his groundbreaking book *Emerging Adulthood*, Arnett describes five qualities that characterize this stage between adolescence and adulthood:

1. *Identity exploration.* Emerging adults are continually seeking to answer the question, Who am I? In an effort

to figure it out, they try different options, particularly with romantic relationships and careers.

2. *Instability.* Change is a big word for emerging adults. Because they are changing majors, partners, jobs, and even residences, instability is part of their experience.

3. *Self-focus.* Emerging adults tend to delay significant adult responsibilities such as marriage and parenthood. With more freedom to explore than they had in adolescence and few of the ties of adulthood, they focus on themselves and their needs and aspirations.

4. *Feeling in-between.* Emerging adults are in transition. When asked if they are adults, they often answer, "Yes and no." They exercise the freedom and lifestyle choices of adulthood, yet they know that they haven't reached full adulthood—marriage, parenting, and job security. Most emerging adults have also been helped financially by their parents.

5. *Possibilities and optimism.* Emerging adults often hold a positive view of the future. They see all the possibilities before them and believe they can avoid making the same mistakes as their parents or loved ones when it comes to relationships and vocation.[7]

As I read Arnett's characteristics of emerging adults, it suddenly made sense why my adult kids act as they do. It was like he was living in our home and listening to our conversations! Just understanding that these are characteristics of this emerging adult generation—rather than quirks of our children—can help us keep the relationship with our children in perspective and perhaps help us to have a bit more patience. I've started using the term adultolescence to describe this stage of life. I know they look like adults, but they still have some latent adolescent traits.

If we aren't attentive to the nuances of our children's changing culture, we can forget that we were raised with a different cultural mindset. Gaining an understanding of why our kids act and think the way they do won't eliminate all the confusion we might have or erase our differing opinions, but it can help us make sense of why they might make choices that shock or surprise us.

THE CRINGE FACTOR

During our HomeWord focus group sessions, there was at least one parent in every group who mentioned the moral freefall they observed in their children and in the young adult culture. I began calling this moral decline the "cringe factor" because the issues are ones that make most parents uncomfortable. To understand emerging adults, we must acknowledge the moral aimlessness of this era. Some emerging adults would no doubt take exception to the phrase "moral aimlessness," but most parents in our focus groups expressed deep concerns about this generation's lack of morals. One parent, who also happened to be a Hollywood movie director, said, "This is the generation in which we experienced the 'death of innocence.'" When I asked him to give me an example, he said, "It's not hard to find troubling trends, but since I have younger kids, how about the fact that the average age of a child's first view of pornography is now eleven years old?" He was right—this generation has lost its innocence, and it affects children's lives well into young adulthood. A loss of innocence sometimes leads to experimentation and behavior that conflicts with morals a child was taught at home. Although this is not a book about every moral issue of the day, I do want to briefly touch on two issues that parents of adult children repeatedly bring up as concerns—pornography and cohabitation.

Pornography

Addiction to pornography almost seems to be the norm for the children of the parents I've talked to. This means we have a whole generation of young people entering adulthood with a distorted view and experience of human sexuality. The pattern that escalates into addiction goes something like this: They view pornography and the images are stored in their minds and biochemically connected with pleasure. They quickly become addicted because their brains are saying, *I want to see more.* Their viewing of porn escalates. Next, they become desensitized, and what was gross or unacceptable a year ago or two months ago isn't gross or unacceptable anymore. The once unacceptable becomes the new norm. The last stage of porn addiction is a willingness to act it out. First, they envision the sex act in their minds, and then they act it out with someone. Many of the first sexual experiences young people now have are an imitation of the porn they viewed. This porn epidemic is changing the way young adults view and engage both physical and emotional intimacy. Of course, the most effective way to combat the use of porn is good and healthy sex education when our kids are young. Experts tell us that the more positive, values-centered sex education kids receive from their parents, the less promiscuous they will tend to be.

Even if you missed the opportunity to give your children a healthy sex education when they were young, you can still come alongside your young adult, but from a different angle. Yes, it's too late to give them the birds and the bees talk, but it's not too late to have an adult-to-adult conversation. I know many parents who were able to bring the right resources at the right time to help their young adult children get the help they needed.

When Bob and Barbie suspected that their son was struggling with an addiction to porn, they did their research and found helpful websites, articles, and treatment programs. Barbie created a resource file, and then she and Bob waited for two years until one day their adult son casually mentioned something about his generation's struggle with porn addiction.

"I can only imagine how hard it would be to be honest enough to seek help," Bob said. "Your mom and I have been keeping a file on helpful resources for people who are struggling with porn addiction. We keep thinking it will come in handy one day if someone from church or anyone we know is seeking help."

Bob did a great job of communicating openness and keeping the subject impersonal. Later that day, their son asked to look at their resource file. Although he didn't tell them he had a problem, he spent the rest of the day reading through the resources his mom had gathered. Many months later, he told his parents that the "pornography resource file" they loaned him had been extremely helpful to him. He found accountability and answers to overcome his addiction, and Bob and Barbie helped in a way that didn't alienate their son.

Cohabitation

The increase in young adults moving in together before marriage has been a dramatic shift. In 2006, the Census Bureau in the United States reported 4.85 million cohabitating couples, up from 439,000 couples in 1960.[8] The percentage of women ages nineteen to forty-four who have ever cohabited has increased by 82 percent over the past twenty-three years.[9]

Although there are a variety of opinions on this subject, many relationship experts who don't disagree with cohabitation on moral or spiritual grounds are nevertheless genuinely concerned about the hidden consequences of cohabitation. For example, according to research by noted Johns Hopkins University sociologist Andrew Cherlin, "Marriages that are preceded by living together have a 50 percent higher disruption rate than marriages without premarital cohabitation."

Other experts indicate that people with cohabitating experience who eventually marry have a 50 to 80 percent higher likelihood of divorcing than married couples who never cohabitated.[10] Couples who cohabitate consistently express a lower level of relational satisfaction than couples who marry. And numerous studies consistently show that cohabitors have much higher levels of sexual infidelity than married couples. According to the research done at the University of California, Irvine, "The odds of a recent infidelity were more than twice as high for cohabitors than for married persons."[11]

Facts are facts and scientific research points to cohabitation as a bad choice.

Cringe factor issues aren't limited to pornography and cohabitation. Many other issues came up in our focus groups as cause for deep parental concern, including gender identity confusion, drug and alcohol use, trouble with the law, extreme political confrontations, and a change in religion or the adoption of atheism, just to name a few complicated issues that make for uncomfortable talk around the holiday dinner table. To navigate these issues and maintain a positive relationship with our children, we need to figure out how to live in what I call "the messy middle."

The messy middle is where we find ourselves when we hold on to a solid moral base that we believe in while loving our kids and others who have chosen a different way. It's not easy for anyone. It's messy. But we can still love our children even when we don't agree with them or approve of their choices. Choosing the messy middle is sometimes confusing but is one of the most effective ways to impact this generation. We'll talk more about how to live in the messy middle shortly, but first we need to tackle one more factor.

THE FAITH FACTOR

Not only has there been a cultural earthquake with various cringe factor issues, but also there has been a seismic shift in how emerging adults view spiritual matters. Fewer are involved in church. According to recent studies, atheism has doubled among those in Generation Z.[12] David Kinnaman's research on emerging adults and Christianity found that both Christian and non-Christian young adults had a negative image of certain issues in the Christian church. Here are some of the words people outside the church used to describe Christianity:[13]

- Antihomosexual: 91 percent
- Judgmental: 87 percent

- Hypocritical: 85 percent
- Too political: 75 percent
- Out of touch with reality: 72 percent
- Insensitive to others: 70 percent
- Boring: 68 percent
- Not accepting of other faiths: 64 percent
- Confusing: 61 percent

Whether these descriptions are true could be debated. But as a parent of adult children, you would probably agree that this is indeed how many emerging adults view the church.

Once again, the way we choose to discuss our faith and values with our young adults is exceedingly important. Do I even need to say that shouting, lecturing, arguing, and preaching simply will not work? They'll run from a lecture, but they are not opposed to a loving, thoughtful discussion in which their opinions are listened to and healthy dialog is created. It's back to the messy middle. We can lovingly disagree with our adult kids, but they do want to be heard.

There are also some positive traits in this generation when it comes to faith and spirituality. Yes, too many are leaving the church after high school, but many of those who leave *do* find their way back once they marry and settle down. There are some wonderful churches having a positive spiritual influence by reaching out to this generation. I often get to speak at some of these churches. While the services look a bit different from traditional ones, the freshness works for a younger generation (and for some of us oldies as well). Biblical truths can still break through to the hearts of emerging adults.

Six Strategies for Keeping Young Adults
Engaged in Their Faith and the Church

My friend Kara Powell and her associates at the Fuller Youth Institute have done a remarkable job researching the spiritual needs of young adults. In the book *Growing Young*, they identify six essential strategies to help young adults remain excited about their faith and involved in the church.

1. *Unlock keychain leadership.* Instead of centralizing authority, empower others—especially young people—to lead. Young adults will support what they help create.
2. *Empathize with today's young people.* Instead of judging or criticizing, step into this generation's shoes. They seek to be understood.
3. *Take Jesus' message seriously.* Instead of asserting doctrines, welcome young people into a Jesus-centered way of life. Extend to them the challenge of following Jesus.
4. *Fuel a warm community.* Instead of focusing on cool worship and programs, aim for warm peer and intergenerational friendships. This is what will keep them in church.
5. *Prioritize young people (and families) everywhere.* Instead of talking about how much young people matter, look for creative ways to support, resource, and involve them in all facets of your faith community. They don't want to be spectators; they want to participate. Otherwise, they'll leave and find something else to participate in.

6. *Be the best neighbors.* Instead of condemning the world beyond the walls of the church, enable young people to neighbor well locally and globally. They identify with the message "the call to Christ is the call to serve."[14]

HOW TO MAINTAIN A POSITIVE RELATIONSHIP IN THE MESSY MIDDLE

Whether our children are struggling with a cringe factor issue or a faith factor issue, there's no question that maintaining a healthy relationship with them can be challenging. One moment we think our adult children are coming at us from a different planet, and the next we see glimpses of hope that they are our children after all. Each child takes a unique road to adulthood, but be assured that with our love and understanding, they will stay in relationship with us. Given the changing cultural mindset, what can we do to maintain a positive relationship while we're in the messy middle? Here are three actions you can take.

1. Meet Them on Their Territory

You don't have to agree with your children to meet them on their territory. Meeting them on their territory means experiencing the world in which they live and by which they are influenced. One year when one of my daughters was eighteen, I asked her to take me to a concert of a band she really liked. I must admit, they were really talented musicians. I didn't love everything about the concert and I didn't agree with some of the words coming out of the mouth of the lead singer, but attending the concert did help me understand who was influencing my kids. More than that, my daughter enjoyed the fact that I was in her territory.

Our adult children will rarely turn us down for a dinner out or a fun experience if we keep our opinions to ourselves and just enjoy their company. As difficult as it can be, sometimes it's best to hold back on the parent-to-child dynamic and try to have more of an adult-to-adult experience. Your adult children do look to you for wisdom and guidance, but they want you to see and understand who they are in their own territory.

I know a couple who recently visited their young adult daughter in Washington, D.C., where she was living. They asked her to plan their four-day visit around whatever she wanted to do and to show them D.C. through her eyes. After the visit with their daughter was over, they admitted they probably wouldn't have chosen the restaurants or sites she showed them, but they considered the visit a success because they had a wonderful time with her and gained great insight into her life. Wise parents.

2. Become a Student of Your Adult Child's Culture

Just as you likely experienced generational differences with your parents, it is natural to experience generational differences with your kids. For example, I was raised in what was once considered a traditional family—my dad worked and my mom stayed at home. My mom's way of showing love was cooking and caring for our home. My mom didn't even know how to use a checkbook. My dad showed his love to our family by working seven days a week. I'm not suggesting that this was the healthiest way of doing life, but it worked for them.

The Living Generations

Understanding the distinctions between the generations often brings clarity to why we think and act the way we do. It's fascinating to see how each generation approaches life and family just a bit differently. Here's a brief overview of how the generations living today are categorized:

- *Elders (born before 1946).* They have been called the greatest generation and the silent generation. They are the traditionalists. They worked hard. Loyalty is a significant value and trait.
- *Baby Boomers (born 1946–1964).* They also have a strong work ethic. They are resourceful, goal oriented, and self-assured.
- *Generation X (born 1965–1983).* This is the MTV generation. They are self-reliant, sometimes cynical, and prone to challenge the status quo.
- *Millennials or Generation Y (born 1984–1998).* They are adventuresome, entrepreneurial, and tied to a digital lifestyle.
- *Generation Z (born 1999–present).* They are known for valuing inclusivity, gender neutrality, and feminism. This generation has moved past Facebook on to Snapchat. Few in this age group will work at the same job their entire career.

When Cathy and I were married, we shared much more of the household chores, Cathy worked outside the home, and Cathy handled our checkbook. None of my adult children even have a checkbook because they use debit cards and pay their bills online. They live and approach relationships differently than my parents did and somewhat differently than Cathy and I do. To understand why they act the way they do, it's important for each generation to recognize some of those differences.

Our job as parents is not to agree with all the values of our children's culture but to have a greater understanding of how culture influences the way they think and act. A broader understanding of their culture will help us communicate and connect with our kids. Becoming aware of generational differences can also help us discern which battles to fight and which ones to let pass. When we avoid the smaller battles, we have a better chance of dealing with the most important ones.

3. Parent with AWE

My mom was a character. By the time we had kids of our own, we called her the "party-time grandma." When you were in Mom's presence, you knew you were loved and accepted, even if she didn't agree with your lifestyle. Mom was born in 1922, so she certainly was part of the elder generation, but people from every generation who knew her loved her and were greatly influenced by her.

Mom has been gone for many years now, but I often reflect on the qualities that enabled her to embrace all generations while still holding firm to her moral compass. Over the years, she collected a variety of people young and old, but it was mostly the young who were drawn to her. She laughed with them. She fed them. She listened to their stories and almost always withheld judgment. They loved her and could never get enough of their time with her. When I was in high school, friends of mine would sometimes drop by the house to ask if I was home. If she said, "He's down at the gym playing basketball," instead of heading to the gym to find me, they'd ask, "Can I just come in and hang out with you, Mrs. Burns?" She always welcomed them in and often fed them some delicious dessert.

It wasn't until she died that I fully realized the secret to her influence and the impact of her life on others. It was simple. She parented and related to the younger generation with a sense of AWE. These three letters stand for affection, warmth, and encouragement. She showered everyone with love, though not necessarily approval of their actions. She bestowed plenty of hugs and words of affection. She welcomed them with sincere warmth. Her tone and demeanor were loving and accepting. She wasn't a student of the culture—she wasn't very cool and certainly not tech savvy. But the young people she encountered knew without doubt that she loved them. She naturally showed love, and when asked for her perspective, she gave it because she had earned the right to be heard.

Today, I keep the letters AWE on my desk to remind me that regardless of what this new generation believes or does, I can give them a huge dose of affection, warmth, and encouragement. And so can you.

Even when there are aspects of our kids' culture we don't understand or can't embrace, we can still move toward developing a positive adult-to-adult relationship. We may have to agree to disagree on certain issues, but that shouldn't stop us from deepening our relationship and investing in meaningful times together. No one said it would be easy, but there is hope for those who persevere.

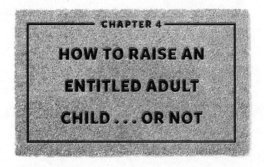

CHAPTER 4

HOW TO RAISE AN ENTITLED ADULT CHILD ... OR NOT

PRINCIPLE 4: THEY WILL NEVER KNOW HOW FAR THE TOWN IS IF YOU CARRY THEM ON YOUR BACK

◆•◆

"I wish my twenty-two-year-old would schedule her own dentist appointments."

‡·‡·‡

In my office sits a handsome young man named Sean, along with his mother and father. Sean has a half smile on his face as if he is almost enjoying the conversation, but his crossed arms also convey some defensiveness. Sean's mom and dad are clearly not happy. His mom is nervous and worried, and I can't tell whether Sean's dad is angrier with his wife or with Sean, but he is obviously frustrated. Sean's mom does most of the talking but constantly looks to her husband for support, which he refuses to give.

Sean's mom describes him as a bright young man who is just out of college. She tells me that he was involved with his fraternity and partying in his college years, that he coasted through school, and that he stretched out a four-year-degree program into six years while his parents covered all of his expenses. After graduation and an extended surfing trip (paid for by his parents), he has been back home for eight months. The presenting problem is that Sean doesn't have much of a job, spends his nights partying with friends, and then sleeps in. His mom and dad are still paying for everything, including his cell phone and Wi-Fi, so Sean has little motivation to get a job. His mom still does his laundry and makes him dinner, often at a different hour than she does for the rest of the family. She even continues to make his bed.

"Sean has a problem!" his mom blurts. This time when she looks to her husband for support, he nods in agreement.

"I don't think Sean has a problem," I say. Everyone, including Sean, stares at me dumbfounded. "I think it's the two of you who have the problem," I say to the parents. "Sean is getting a pretty sweet deal. If you want him to become a responsible adult, give him some boundaries and expectations. Set a timeline starting right now to get him off your family payroll."

Sean quit smiling.

ARE YOU ENABLING YOUR ADULT CHILD OR HELPING?

The question Sean's parents needed to ask themselves is, "Are we helping Sean to become a responsible adult, or are we enabling him to remain an irresponsible adolescent?" Our behavior is enabling when we do for others what they can and need to do for themselves. Here is how the Hazelden Betty Ford Foundation distinguishes enabling from helping: "Enabling behavior, simply put, shields people from experiencing the full impact and consequences of their behavior. Enabling is different from helping and supporting in that it allows the enabled person to be irresponsible."[15]

It's not hard to recognize this dynamic in the relationship between Sean and his parents. Enabling creates an environment in which an adult child can comfortably continue with unacceptable behavior. If you are always trying to ease your adult children's pain or protect them from hardship, you only make them more dependent on you. In her book *Setting*

Boundaries with Your Adult Children, author Allison Bottke writes, "Self-awareness of the part we play in the enabling dynamic is a major success step."[16] If we aren't aware of our part in the enabling process, our children may not reach the goal of responsible adulthood. If Sean's parents couldn't recognize their part in enabling in his poor decisions, then Sean would keep on living just like he had been. This doesn't mean we don't ever help our kids. That's an important part of parenting. We just can't always be bailing them out.

My friends Bob and Cheryl are a perfect example of helping and empowering rather than enabling adult kids. They raised their three children in a loving Christian home and instilled strong values and a biblical mindset into their family. When their college-age daughter Amanda was pulled over by a police officer and arrested for driving under the influence of alcohol, Bob and Cheryl were crushed. They couldn't believe their daughter would make such a poor choice. But they also believed Amanda was fundamentally a good person who had made a serious error in judgment. They took into consideration that her blood alcohol level was barely above the limit and decided to support her, but not to shield her.

Bob and Cheryl easily could have afforded the best DUI attorney to get their daughter off with a slap on the wrist, but they chose not to do that. After considerable conversation and prayer, they decided it was best for their daughter to experience the full weight of the consequences of her behavior. This meant having her driver's license revoked for one year, attending DUI school (which was humiliating for the young adult), paying increased insurance rates for ten years, and keeping a DUI on her record for ten years. That was nearly ten years ago, and so Amanda's consequences will soon be ending. When I asked Bob and Cheryl if they had any regrets about their decision, they said, "Absolutely not. Letting her learn the 'you reap what you sow' principle was more important than bailing her out." Amanda never repeated her mistake, and she now has a much healthier appreciation for the consequences of her choices, in large part because her parents didn't shield her from the outcome of her actions.

Although it's natural to want to protect our children, we must break the enabling habit. Enabling produces only entitlement and dependence, and our goal is always to help our children move toward full maturity and independence. In John Townsend's wonderful book *The Entitlement Cure*, he writes, "There is a right way to live, and it is the Hard Way. It is work, but it *works*, and it will save you countless detours in life."[17] The hard way Townsend refers to means not taking shortcuts or the easy way out. It's choosing instead to make the often difficult choice to work on what's most important and what will bring the greatest results. Enabling produces entitlement, but setting clear boundaries and expectations produces healthy responsibility.

NEGOTIATING BOUNDARIES

Being a good parent of a young adult requires establishing healthy boundaries for our kids and then holding them accountable. The goal in moving toward responsible adulthood is to take the monkey of responsibility off your back and place it squarely on the back of your adult child. This goes right along with the saying "They will never know how far the town is if you carry them on your back."

Nuggets of Wisdom about Setting Boundaries

Here are some helpful phrases to remember about setting boundaries:

- *"You earned it."* In other words, "You earned your negative outcome and consequences." This is the principle that you reap what you sow. It's often used in the recovery movement with alcohol and drug abusers, but it also works well when setting and enforcing healthy boundaries. When adult children make poor choices, we can say they earned their consequences. That our behaviors have consequences is an essential lesson for adolescents and young adults.
- *"You can choose the pain of self-discipline or the pain of regret."* Everyone knows there is pain in life. We choose either the pain of self-discipline or the pain of living with regrets. Enabling our adult children takes away the opportunity for them to grow in self-discipline.
- *You can't want it more than they want it.* If your kids don't want to make good choices, no amount of wanting them to on your part will change things. Even when our adult children aren't making good decisions or have made a mess of their lives, we must let them clean up their messes. There are consequences for our choices, both good and bad. Until your kids decide they want good consequences, you can't want them into good choices.

- *When the pain of remaining the same is greater than the pain of changing, they will change.* One parent said to me, "I knew my daughter was making some poor choices. I also knew that when the pain threshold of her decisions got to a breaking point, she had the skills to make better decisions." It seems like most of life's lessons come through the school of hard knocks. Sometimes adult kids learn best through the pain of poor choices.

Negotiating boundaries can be extremely tough, but the saying is true, "Good fences make good neighbors." Boundaries give your adult children an opportunity to thrive by providing a structure for healthy independence. Some might ask, "Can I set boundaries and still be a loving parent?" The answer is a resounding yes! Establishing boundaries is not selfish or unloving but rather the best way to give your children the wings to become responsible adults. If you take on responsibilities your adult children should be carrying, you only perpetuate an unhealthy dependency that keeps your kids from making healthy lifestyle choices. In creating appropriate boundaries, you are living out the biblical mandate, "Each one should carry their own load" (Gal. 6:5). Everyone has responsibilities that only he or she can rightly carry. Boundaries are a loving way to create a path toward responsibility for one's actions. To negotiate healthy boundaries with your adult child, you need to do two things: express expectations clearly and develop an action plan.

Express Expectations Clearly

After college, Julie moved to a different part of the country. She hoped to get a job, find a roommate, and begin living as a responsible adult. Her parents, John and Olivia, were proud of her college graduation and eager to help her make the transition to independence. They said they would help pay for her first month's rent and move-in expenses and continue paying for her car and health insurance, as well as give her an allowance for a few months until she got a job. One month later, everything changed when she moved in with a new boyfriend. Cohabitation was not what John and Olivia hoped for with their daughter.

They flew out to see her and get their arms around the situation. They were not happy or impressed with her decision, but they expressed their concern with love. The conversation was awkward, but Julie knew and understood their values. The hardest part of the conversation was when John and Olivia had to tell their daughter that even though they disapproved of her decision, they knew there was nothing they could do about it. Their daughter had emphatically told them more than once that she was an adult and could live as she wanted.

"Yes, it's true," John said. "You are an adult, and we want to treat you with all the love and respect an adult deserves. With adulthood comes responsibility, so we assume you can pay your own rent, car, and health insurance and that you no longer need an allowance." These words were spoken factually, not in anger or as a punishment. Both John and Olivia affirmed that their love for her was just as strong as ever. A few months later, the relationship with the boyfriend ended and Julie asked if she could move home for a few months. Her parents lovingly welcomed her back.

As hard as it was, John and Olivia did several things right:

- Even though their hearts were breaking, they continued to show love and did not sever the relationship.
- They didn't become one-topic parents, focused only on what was wrong with their daughter's decision.
- They let her know how they felt about her choices and what they believed, but kept the relationship strong by affirming their love for her.
- They allowed her to live with the consequences of her choices.
- They clearly expressed their love and expectations.

Believe it or not, many adult children tell me that their parents never clearly expressed their expectations. Perhaps they were hinted at or implied, but not clearly expressed. Conversations about boundaries and expectations can be awkward, but we must have them. The more clearly we express our expectations, the better things will be in the relationship.

Expectations must be tailored to fit the needs and circumstances of your adult child. There is no one size fits all. One couple told me their expectations were different even for their twin sons, one of whom was in college and the other of whom was in the military. Expectations will also differ depending on whether your adult child lives in your home. An adult child struggling with an addiction or a mental illness will, of course, require boundaries tailored to the situation.

I often suggest that parents create a simple contract of understanding, especially if an adult child is still in the home, or receiving some form of financial support. This is just an informal document that simply states the agreed-upon expectations. Some families write them out, and others just discuss them. However you do it, the expectations must be clear and the consequences even clearer. One parent I know wrote a contract that began with these words: "You are welcome to stay, but . . ." She then filled in her list of expectations. Regardless of how you express your expectations, make sure you have an exit plan. An exit plan is a strategy to help your adult child transition toward adult responsibility. Keep that objective in mind.

Here are some key points I would include in a contract:

EXPECTATIONS

- *"Be productive."* Spell out what you mean by being productive. For example, have a job, attend school, share responsibilities in the home, and so on.
- *"Honor our moral standards in our home."* You can't micromanage them or enforce behavior outside the home, but you can choose what happens in your home.
- *"Be financially responsible."* Young adults need to be accountable for as much of their finances as possible and need to be moving toward total responsibility. If they get an allowance from you and are not working but are still enjoying eating out and other nonessential expenditures, that's not becoming financially responsible.
- *"Be an active member of our family."* When one of our daughters moved back home, we told her this was not the Burns Hotel and she was responsible for helping with household chores. Our good friends handed their son a bucket and scrub brush and said, "Now that you are back home, you have 'cleaning the toilet' duty." Others might

ask for something such as having at least one dinner together a week.

- *"This is the timeline and these are the goals you need to meet to be on your own."* Develop the timeline and goals together with your adult child and be clear about your mutually desired outcome. For example, we know a family who helped their daughter make a transition over a six-month period. During that time, they offered limited financial assistance. By the end of the six months, their daughter was ready to take on full financial responsibilities. They celebrated with a wonderful dinner together and then blessed her with a financial gift to give her a boost with her first month's rent for her new apartment.

CONSEQUENCES

- *"Rent is free as long as you are being financially responsible and productive. If you aren't, then we will start charging rent."* Some parents charge rent in addition to expecting financial responsibility in other areas. Do what best serves your child and helps him or her to move toward independence.
- *"If you won't honor the moral standards of our home, you have the right to move out."* Some parents have trouble with "putting their kids out in the street." You don't have to make this a dramatic event. It's simply a natural consequence of an adult child's not wanting to live by your home guidelines. Some might say, "Yes, but what if they move in with their boyfriend or girlfriend or do more drugs?" By allowing behavior in your home that goes

against your morals and values, you really aren't helping your child become responsible, and he or she is already doing it anyway. Sometimes saying I love you requires tough love.

- *"We expect your chores to be done in a timely manner or it means you are ready to move out."* Too many times, adult children avoid the tasks and chores that would be naturally expected of them. They would have to do dishes and make their beds if they were on their own. Treat them as adults and expect them to share in reasonable responsibilities at home. Make sure the expectations are clear.

For their sake as well as yours, follow through with consequences. Remember, there is a huge difference between punishment and consequences. Punishment is about making your kids suffer for their mistakes by inflicting pain or making them feel bad. Punishment most often causes resentment and rarely teaches the lesson you want them to learn. Consequences, on the other hand, help people learn and grow. Consequences flow naturally out of one's decisions and actions. Natural and logical consequences teach us how to do it better next time.

You aren't punishing your child when you enforce consequences. In life, there are consequences for our actions, so it should seem normal and natural to create consequences for failure to meet your expectations. Whenever possible, create the consequences with your child. If consequences are imposed rather than agreed upon, there is a higher likelihood of resentment or a complicated mix of emotions that could damage the relationship.

Cathy and I have a close relative we love dearly who moved in with his girlfriend shortly after graduating college several years ago. Our children were younger at the time. One day, this relative called to ask if he and his girlfriend could visit for a weekend. We were thrilled to have them. It wasn't our job to force our moral values on them, but we felt it necessary to ask them to sleep in separate rooms while staying in our home. I called him back and simply said, "We are excited you are coming for a visit. I hope you don't mind, but we will need to ask you to sleep separately during your visit." I'm sure he knew our values. He took it graciously and nothing more needed to be said. If your children or relatives choose not to live by your values outside your home, there really isn't much you can do. They may be compromising the values they learned from you when they are on their own, but you still have a right to create boundaries and expectations for your home.

Expressing our expectations is a way of providing leadership for our children, whatever their age. Great leaders are easy to follow because they lead with love, compassion, and integrity. I want to be a man of integrity. A proverb in the Bible states, "Whoever walks in integrity walks securely" (Prov. 10:9). Integrity doesn't mean perfection but rather means consistency of character. It's that consistency that enables us to lead our children into responsible adulthood. Sometimes that means not taking the easy route. Some parents have indulged and enabled their children to such an extent that they have helped to create irresponsible and even narcissistic adults.

Sometimes, the first thing we need to do when adult children make poor choices is to take a hard look at our behavior. Are we softening the consequences of their choices? A responsible adult child pays back a loan or abides by the moral code of the family home. If we set out expectations and then don't follow

through with consequences, we are partly responsible for
negative outcome. One friend of ours said, "If you think par
ing a teen is hard, wait until they are thirty-five and move b
in with two kids and a lifestyle that is contrary to yours."
described how hard it was for him and his wife to shower th
daughter with love and grace while maintaining leadership
the home.

"We had to do some deep soul-searching to reevaluate
behavior and feelings about this new situation," he said. "\
realized that we were a bit shellshocked from our daughter m
ing in with her kids, but we needed to provide leadership a
create some expectations for our daughter, who, at the mome
was almost immobilized with grief over her circumstances."

Here's another thing to keep in mind. Your kids might ac
ally appreciate it when you express your expectations. Wh
Brent and Tiffany sat down with their son to create some expe
tations about his moving back home, they thought it might
poorly. It didn't. Their son appreciated the communication ar
being a part of creating expectations. Brent and Tiffany said the
were a few parts of the discussion that got a bit emotional but th
outcome was clear and good. After having a good conversatio
about expectations, they created a plan together to help their so
achieve full adult responsibility by moving out on his own.

Develop an Action Plan

Once you've expressed your expectations, the next step is to mak
an action plan to move your adult child from dependence to inde
pendence. An action plan may sound businesslike or out of place
in a family context, but having a plan is one of the most effective
ways to help your adult children take their next steps, especially

if they are still living with you or relying on you financially. I've never met a family who regretted making an action plan. It's an essential component of expressing expectations, building boundaries, and following through on consequences. An action plan doesn't have to be super formal or detailed, but having a written plan is more effective than just talking about it.

For Brent and Tiffany, creating an action plan for their son was easy because they had already done the work of creating expectations together. They asked their son to think about what he would like to do as he prepared to transition out of the home to financial independence, and then to set a timeframe for moving out. To their surprise and delight , when they met, he handed them a well-thought-out plan and even included some consequences if he failed to reach his goals. Brent's comment was, "Wow! That was a lot easier than I thought it was going to be." Brent and Tiffany added a few thoughts to the plan, but now all the issues had been discussed and the three of them were on the same page.

Here are a few guidelines to help you create a simple action plan:

- *Begin with the end in mind.* The goal is responsible and independent adulthood. The goal for your action plan is whatever needs to happen for your adult child to become fully responsible for his or her life. For example, "My plan is to have a full-time job that pays for all my expenses—including my college tuition loan—and to move to my own apartment by June 30."
- *Set deadlines.* Set deadlines to achieve objectives, and set dates to review progress and address challenges.

Specifying a date or timeframe works much better than agreeing on something vague like "in a few months" or "by the summer." You can always change the deadline if you need to.

- *Establish consequences.* There need to be consequences for failing to meet agreed-upon goals and deadlines. Work with your adult child to establish what those consequences should be.

Be sure to create the action plan with your child. People are much more likely to support something they helped to create.

I love the proverb that says, "Where there is no vision, the people perish" (Prov. 29:18 KJV). Developing an action plan is a way to give your adult child both a compelling vision and a roadmap for their journey from dependence to responsible adulthood. It helps both of you to focus your relationship on shared goals and gives them the confidence they need to move forward.

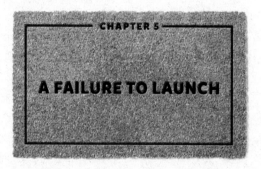

CHAPTER 5

A FAILURE TO LAUNCH

PRINCIPLE 5: YOUR JOB IS TO MOVE THEM FROM DEPENDENCE TO INDEPENDENCE

"And the thing is, Mom and Dad, I've lived upstairs since I was three, and it's been great."

—TRIPP, AGE THIRTY-FIVE

"What we have here is a failure to launch."

—AL, TRIPP'S DAD

ꓕ·ꓕ·ꓕ

Have you ever seen the comedy *Failure to Launch*? Matthew McConaughey and Sarah Jessica Parker star in this movie about thirty-five-year-old Tripp, who still enjoys living with his parents. His parents, however, want him out. In his dad's words, "He's thirty-five years old. He still lives in the house. This is not normal!"

Tripp, played by McConaughey, says to his friends, "It would take a stick of dynamite to get me out of my parents' home." Even his friends think it's a bit weird that he hasn't moved out. "Do you sleep well at night?" one of them asks. "Yes," Tripp says with a smile. His best friend adds, "But you sleep on a twin bed with Superman sheets that you have had since you were six years old." His parents end up hiring Paula, a motivator-interventionist played by Sarah Jessica Parker, in the hope of graduating Tripp out of the house, and that's when all the fun begins.

Not since the 1940s have so many adult children lived at home. And today, it is much more normal for adult children to move back home after having left. This, of course, is not always a bad thing. There are several reasons kids move home or are out of the house but still get financial help from their parents.

One of our daughters had been living on her own when her roommate moved, and she decided to go to graduate school to get a degree in clinical psychology. She asked to move home so she could save money for grad school.

Although Cathy and I had to quickly make some mental and emotional adjustments, we felt it was a good idea, and we loved having her back. She moved back to the same house she'd grown up in, but we now had a different family structure. She'd left home for college as a kid but was returning as an adult. Everyone needed to adjust. At first, Cathy and I found ourselves reverting to the parental patterns and behaviors we'd followed when she was a teenager. We had to adjust our expectation of when she came home at night and stop asking her whether she'd finished her school work. She was an adult and was paying for her own graduate degree. Cathy and I had to say, "That was then, and this is now." Our daughter also had to step up to adulthood and take on some new responsibilities, such as helping with work around the house and communicating whether she was coming home for dinner, that would have seemed foreign to her before she left for college.

Kids who move back home or stay on their parents' bankroll are called "boomerang kids." Whereas young adults in previous generations might have considered moving back home a last resort, young adults today tend to see it as simply a part of their path toward independence. Some boomerangers view their stay as temporary, and others are late bloomers or are so comfortable in the family home that they don't really have much of an exit plan. Whatever their reasons for returning or staying, incorporating an adult child into a family living situation is often complicated. My friends Bill and Kristen found out just how complicated it could be when they were only a few years into their new marriage and Kristen's young-adult daughter from a previous marriage moved in with them. Bill had not raised his stepdaughter, and he was already used to the empty nest. Having Kristen's daughter in their home didn't go well. It almost cost Bill and Kristen their marriage.

Both parents and their adult children tell me that a child's moving back home often creates a muddled mix of issues. For example, parents often talk about the panic they feel late at night when their adult child is not yet home. Of course, when their child was away at college or out on their own, they no longer had a curfew, and they don't see the need to go back to having one. The parents panic and get angry, while the adult child just can't understand why they "freak out" over something as trivial as later hours. Young adults complain that their parents treat them as children, and parents complain that their kids *act* like children. Parents are often frustrated that their adult child isn't moving toward independence, but kids sometimes don't see why they should when they can enjoy the comforts of a big screen TV, a fully stocked refrigerator, home-cooked meals, and laundry facilities, all at no charge.

Old habits die hard. When kids move back home, many parents rediscover their "need" for control, especially if their parenting style is what some describe as "helicopter parenting."

LAND THE HELICOPTER

The term helicopter parent was coined in 1969 by Dr. Haim Ginott in his book *Between Parent and Teenager*. It refers to a parent who hovers or "helicopters" over their child and is overprotective or overinvested in the life of that child. It starts when the kids are young but sometimes continues into young adulthood. For example, helicopter parents might call their college-age child to remind her to get up in time for class or to see whether she's completed her homework. If that sounds farfetched, consider this. A friend of mine who is a college president told me about a conversation he had with a parent who called him to complain that her son had gotten a D on a paper in a business class. She wanted to have the grade changed. My friend later followed up with the professor who'd given the grade. The professor remembered the paper and said, "Actually, it was closer to an F than a D." When the college president called the mother back and reported what the professor said, she became angry. "I totally disagree," she said. "I have an MBA from Stanford University and I wrote that paper for my son!" I think she missed both the point and the irony of her statement. And helicopter parents wonder why their kids feel entitled and aren't launching?

It's time to land the helicopter! A hovering parent is not good for an adult child, and hovering is not good for the parent either. It's important to distinguish between caring *for* them and taking care *of* them. Caring for them means you are showering them with healthy nurture and love while allowing them to become independent of you. But taking care of them means you are reverting to the first two decades of your child's life, when they were more dependent on you and your responsibility was to protect them. One recovering helicopter parent said, "I had to stop pushing my kids on issues they don't seem to get. If it's important, life will teach them that lesson." Caring for an adult child is a good thing; taking care of them is not.

Overly protective parents often refuse to let go not because their *kids* have needs but because *they* have needs. Specifically, they need to be needed. This leads them to encourage dependency. We exercised power and control when we raised our toddlers, and rightly so, but parental power and control are the last things our adult children need from us. Such helicoptering holds them back from being all they were meant to be. Parents who continue to take care of their adult sons and daughters out of their own need to be needed do so at the expense of their adult children's maturity. They often also end up sacrificing their own well-being, their financial security, or the health of their marriage. Helicopter parenting is a lose-lose scenario.

To land the helicopter safely requires parents to hold fast to healthy boundaries and to refrain from coddling and taking care of their adult children. The Optimum Performance Institute specializes in working with young adults and their parents who experience what they call the "failure to launch syndrome." Here are their guidelines for landing the helicopter:

- Do not cook, clean, or do laundry for them on a regular basis.
- When they're struggling to find the solution to a problem, sit back and let them find it.
- Do not let them live with you if they are not contributing to the household.
- Require your unemployed child to seek work or further education in order to stay in the family home.
- Do not pay their way; adult children should be required to pay for their own gas, food, and clothing.[18]

When I present these guidelines to parents, I receive mixed reactions. Although most parents understand that following them will help launch their children toward responsible adulthood, others offer up some lame excuses:

- "But my son never learned to cook. He'll starve or waste his money on junk food."
- "She does her laundry wrong, and if I let her do it, she will ruin her clothes."
- "We want her in a safe car, so we pay for it, along with insurance and gas. It's really just a safety issue."

I get it. Life is complicated. Nevertheless, we can't help our kids launch in a healthy manner if we continue to do it all for them. One helicopter parent asked me, "How can I miss my son if he won't go away?" My response was, "Why would he want to go away? He is getting a great deal at home with your doing it all for him."

Author C. S. Lewis once said, "Change always involves a sense of loss." Cathy and I have conflicting feelings about our girls growing up. We know we are no longer in the forefront of their minds as they are in ours, and that's how it should be. We know that for them to thrive, they need to move away from us emotionally, spiritually, and physically. Even so, it's not easy. When each of our girls started talking about moving out of state, we realized we had to grieve this potential loss to our lives and mourn some of our dreams. Maturity often requires making adjustments to our hopes, dreams, and lifestyles. On the one hand, we wanted our kids to become fully functioning adults, but on the other hand, we still thought of them as children who needed and depended on us. As our kids transitioned into young adulthood, we often needed to be reminded of the developmental process psychologists call "individuation."

THE IMPORTANCE OF INDIVIDUATION

When a child is born, that child is totally dependent on his or her parents for survival. The bond that takes place is quite amazing. I remember telling one of my daughters that the day she was born, a piece of my heart was taken from me and placed squarely in her heart. From that day on, I was never the same. I would have died for her. But as strong as that bond is, an inevitable and essential part of a healthy parent-child relationship is moving the child from dependence to independence.

In their bestselling book *Boundaries*, psychologists Henry Cloud and John Townsend describe the healthy and necessary process of individuation and separating from parents as "the child's need to perceive himself or herself as distinct from mother, a 'not me' experience." I like how they sum it up: "You can't have 'me' until you first have a 'not-me.'"[19] Cathy and I experienced this process with all three of our girls, but I especially remember one experience that marked the transition for our oldest daughter. When she was just graduating from college, she wrote an article for the school newspaper that included this statement: "I had to disown my parents' faith to begin to own my own faith." Those were hard words for us to hear, but then we realized that this was a healthy move of individuation in her faith.

Jesus made a compelling statement about individuation when he said, "A man will leave his father and mother and be united to his wife, and the two will become one flesh" (Matt. 19:5). You can't have a successful marital relationship if you are still tied to your parents' apron strings. This need to leave parents is key to healthy individuation. For young adults to experience maturity and autonomy, they need to leave emotionally, spiritually, and physically. So the individuation process requires something of both the adult child and the parent. The adult child needs to leave to become mature and responsible, and the parent must release the adult child to become an independent person. This process rarely happens without a few bumps and bruises.

Each stage of parenting has its set of joys and challenges. From potty training to dealing with a troubled teen, we may sometimes think there could not be a more confusing or difficult stage than the one we're in. Yet for many parents, it's this final stage of trying to balance care and concern with respect for privacy and individuation that truly is the most difficult stage of all. The natural distancing from parents that takes place in young adulthood comes as a shock to parents, although they probably engaged in the same distancing with their own parents. When communication is reduced—sending fewer texts, keeping things private, not sharing information about friends or who they might be dating—this stage of parenting can be both painful and confusing. Parents who spend nearly two decades knowing virtually everything there is to know about their child suddenly feel left in the dark. As hard as it may be when this happens, it probably means your child is on the road to healthy individuation.

What can a parent do to help the process? Here is some practical wisdom drawn from focus groups and hundreds of conversations with parents of adult children:

- *Strong criticism and judgmental statements paralyze growth.* Sometimes a critical or judging parent becomes a critical and judgmental voice in an adult child's thinking. With constant criticism or a feeling of judgment, their only choice is to flee from their parents' input or become dependent on their parents. Neither option is the best outcome.

- *Change your role from parent-child to adult-adult.* This is an important theme we've explored throughout this book, but it's key to the individuation process as well. This transition is seldom easy or fun, but it is the only way to a healthy relationship.

- *Cheer on their progress toward adult responsibility.* This will help move your adult child toward maturity and independence. It's important for your child to know how you feel about them. Clearly demonstrate your respect and give plenty of praise and affirmation. Affirmation is almost always more powerful than criticism in helping to create positive change.

- *Allow your adult children to control the amount of time they spend with you.* Allow them to initiate a chance to connect. You can help your adult child create healthy and needed boundaries by giving them some space. At the same time, if there is a need to talk with them, a statement like "I know you are busy, but give me a call when you can" helps them to see that you value their commitment to other responsibilities as well.

- *Stop accommodating your children.* Don't do for them what they can do for themselves. Even if they don't do it as well as you can, let them do it. You have had a lot more experience. They need experience.

- *Encourage hope.* In everything you do, give them hope. Keep in mind that for many adult children, stepping into adult responsibility is a tough decision. They may have a lot of unspoken worries and doubts. The more hope you provide, the easier the transition will be.

The healthiest form of moving from dependence toward independence is the path of individuation. It's a lifelong process toward wholeness. We need to look at it not so much as breaking away from the family as a rite of passage toward deeper personal growth and wholeness with the entire family. Some people have compared the process of individuation to the growth of an oak tree. It is born of a single acorn, but it takes years (truly a lifetime) to become a fully grown and mature oak tree.

VIEW EMERGING ADULTHOOD AS A RITE OF PASSAGE

One of the things I find fascinating about many cultures is the way they celebrate rites of passage from childhood to manhood and womanhood. Perhaps the most well-known coming-of-age ceremony is the Jewish rite of a bar mitzvah for boys and a bat mitzvah for girls. Celebrated when the child turns thirteen, these ceremonies publicly recognize that the child has become an adult. They are now considered fully accountable for their actions and entitled to participate as adults in all religious rituals and legal proceedings. Of course, when this tradition began, there was no such concept as adolescence, and these kids were considered adults. The usual age for marriage under the Jewish

Why Blessing Your Children with a Rite
of Passage Matters So Much

Several years ago, I did a lot of conference speaking with an organization called Promise Keepers. It was a movement that brought together millions of men with the goal of encouraging and equipping them to grow spiritually and to become God-honoring husbands, fathers, and leaders. My friend Randy Phillips was the president of Promise Keepers, and I was always amazed at how a simple statement he made elicited such a strong emotional response. He said, "A man is not a man until his father says he is." Men in the audience often cried or expressed sadness and regret. Too many had gone from childhood to adulthood without any acknowledgment or affirmation from their fathers (or mothers). For them, there was no rite of passage to manhood. A simple act of recognition from either parent, but perhaps especially from a father, would have meant a great deal to these men. It also may have helped some who struggled to rise to the occasion and be more responsible in their young adult years.

This need for a rite of passage—to be honored and affirmed at this important stage in one's life—is not exclusive to young men. As our daughters become young women, we also need to recognize and celebrate them.

---

law at the time of Jesus was between twelve and fourteen. Most scholars believe that Mary, the mother of Jesus, was most likely between these ages when she became pregnant. Whether or not it's marked by a ceremony, the age of accountability in most Western cultures today typically falls somewhere between the ages of seventeen and twenty-one.

A few years ago, I coauthored a book called *Pass It On,*[20] which aims to help parents leave a legacy for their children by celebrating a specific rite of passage each year of a child's life from kindergarten to twelfth grade. After the book was published, I heard many parents' wonderful stories of the meaningful ceremonies and experiences they'd created and the symbols they had given to their children to mark their passage from one age to the next. Not too long ago, I was even invited to attend one of these ceremonies.

To mark Justin's transition from childhood to adulthood, his parents threw him a special party on his eighteenth birthday. They invited people who had been involved in his life and asked them to come prepared to share a short piece of advice or wisdom with Justin. This family knew how to throw a party, and it was a joyous occasion, complete with one of the best barbecue spreads I have ever seen.

After everyone had eaten, Justin's father gathered us all together. It was a beautiful sight to see all the men and women who had spoken into Justin's life, including a coach, a youth pastor, relatives, and friends. His mom and dad presented him with a gift that signified and affirmed his transition to adulthood. We then went around the room and each person imparted advice, shared a story, or read something meaningful and personal. A few times, I must admit, I teared up, and I wasn't the only one. It was a moving and powerful evening of fun, celebration, and blessing.

As the evening was coming to a close, Justin thanked his

parents and said, "This is a day I will never forget." No doubt on that day he was not yet fully mature or ready for complete independence, but these wise parents understood the significance of marking the moment and celebrating their son with a rite of passage that got him off to a great start. And it was just as important for Justin's parents as it was for Justin. It affected them in several areas: their marriage, their finances, and their future.

Although most of us don't have a formal ceremony, every parent must find a way to release their child and to recognize his or her passage to adulthood. It's difficult to release your child at any time, but sometimes it's in the releasing—which tends to be a continual process rather than a onetime experience—that we experience renewed hope and comfort. That was certainly the case for Justin's parents. When they recognized Justin's entrance to manhood, it reminded them of the incredible legacy of great leaders, fathers, and husbands who had gone before him in their family tree. For another family without a positive family history, a rite of passage could mark a transitional generation that not only sets up the adult child to make better choices in adulthood but also starts a new family legacy.

When to Create a Rite of Passage
Experience for Your Adult Child

When kids are younger, it's easier to celebrate their rites of passage, such as moving from grade school to junior high, getting a driver's license, or even entering puberty. Parents can celebrate a rite of passage with younger kids by giving a symbolic gift, hosting a celebration, and including a ceremony to enhance the celebration. Celebrating young adults might include a special meal and a symbolic gift, but not a major ceremony.

Here are a few transitional times you might use as occasions to celebrate a rite of passage for your adult child:

- Moving away to college
- College graduation
- Military enlistment
- First full-time job
- Job promotion or change
- Engagement party
- Marriage
- Birth of a baby
- Buying a first home
- Special occasions with grandchildren, such as baptisms, dedications, and spiritual commitments. As a grandparent, you can make such rites of passage meaningful for your adult children as well as your grandchildren.

Some parents have told me that helping their adult child launch into responsible adulthood was the easiest thing they had ever experienced, and others have told me they are still wondering whether it will ever happen. There are no formulas or easy answers. But once you've helped your kids become mature and responsible adults, you've done your job. Now they need to do their job.

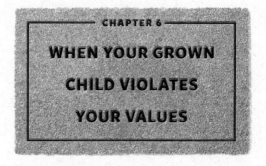

CHAPTER 6

WHEN YOUR GROWN CHILD VIOLATES YOUR VALUES

PRINCIPLE 6: YOU CAN'T WANT IT MORE THAN THEY WANT IT

"Good thing Easter is a season and not just a day, because some resurrections take time."

I was sitting outside on a bench at a conference center in Connecticut getting ready to speak to a large group of parents when the phone call came in. I knew my friend was going to call, but I had no idea why. He asked if I had time. "Only fifteen minutes," I said.

"Yesterday, I received a call from my twenty-one-year-old daughter," he said. "Before she said anything else, she asked me if I was sitting down. I knew that wasn't a good sign. There was a long, awkward pause and then she said, 'Dad, I'm going to get married. I know you won't approve, but I'm going to do it anyway. Mom approves.'" My friend and his wife had been divorced for several years after his wife left him for another woman. "Then she said, 'And Dad, the person is forty-two years old.'

"I tried to keep my cool," he said, "so I responded, 'Wow, that's quite an age difference. How long have you known him?' Which is when I learned why she'd asked if I was sitting down. She said, 'I've only known *her* for two months, but I know it's love.'" At this point in our conversation, he lost his composure and started to cry. Then he added, "My daughter invited me to her wedding, which is two weeks from now. She told me the service would be a bit 'nontraditional' and that I wouldn't be walking her down the aisle."

I knew the dad well enough to know he was heartbroken on several levels. The situation brought back the deep pain and sense of failure from his marriage, plus his values were different from his daughter's. I looked at my watch and realized I had only ten minutes before I had to end the conversation.

"Does your daughter know you love her, and does she know how you feel about her decision?"

He gave me an emphatic yes to both questions.

Realizing this was not a counseling session but a friend asking for my input, I said, "If she were my daughter, I would attend the wedding. I would no doubt be heartbroken, confused, and dismayed, but my presence at her wedding would convey my love without giving my approval."

Near the end of our brief conversation, I added, "I'm going to guess that there will be a crash in the relationship. Getting married after knowing anyone for only two months is seldom a good idea, not to mention that you said she broke up with her boyfriend just two months ago. The odds point toward divorce."

We discussed the fact that *when* she crashed, she would need someone to turn to for help. I encouraged him not to break the relationship over her poor decision but to let her know he was there for her if she ever needed help.

Sure enough, a few months after the wedding, she called her dad and said she was leaving the relationship and asked if she could move back home. She wanted to get her life straightened out. After a couple of years, she's now in a much better situation. She got the counseling help she needed and started attending her father's church, where she found a loving and accepting community. She experienced some bumps and bruises, but I believe her dad's decision to show up at the wedding and to maintain their relationship was a significant factor in her redemptive story.

EVEN GOOD PARENTS HAVE CHILDREN WHO MAKE POOR CHOICES

When an adult child violates our values, makes poor choices, or gets in deep trouble, we often question our parenting abilities. Our doubts shout at us:

- Was it something I did?
- Would this have happened if I'd been a better parent?
- Would this have happened if I had been more spiritual, or if we had prayed more as a family?
- Would this have happened if my marriage hadn't failed?
- Would this have happened if we hadn't argued so much?

The what-ifs can paralyze our souls and wreak havoc on our confidence as parents.

One of the greatest heartbreaks for a parent is watching a child waste his or her life, potential, or opportunities with poor choices. One woman said to me, "I've been through a lot of pain in my life, but I've never felt heartbreak like I have through the poor choices of my kids." A friend of mine whose son struggled with drug and sex addictions put it this way: "It feels like a death. Or at least the death of a dream. No doubt about it, 'big children bring on bigger problems.'"

When your young-adult kids have serious adult-sized problems, the kind that can derail a healthy and productive life, your heart may break, but your child's choices don't have to break you. Your child's regrettable decisions do not make you a bad parent. Even good parents have children who make poor choices.

It may be too late for prevention, but it's never too late for redemption. Miracles do happen. Sometimes they take the form of a rapid change, but most times they are a slow climb toward a better life. Author C. S. Lewis wrote, "Hardship often prepares an ordinary person for an extraordinary destiny." Your child's failures may well become the foundation for a whole new life. This is the power of redemption.

There is perhaps no more powerful story of redemption than Jesus' story about a prodigal or lost son. It's a tragedy that ends with a victory. I'm guessing you already know the story, but every parent of a child who's made regrettable choices needs to be reminded of it.

A father had two sons, and the younger son left home and lived a life contrary to the values of his family. He traveled to a distant country and squandered all his money in what Jesus described as "wild living" (Luke 15:13). When a famine hit, the son ended up with the only job he could find, which was feeding pigs, the kind of job no good Jewish boy would ever take. Finally, he came to his senses and set out for home.

The boy's father had no doubt been brokenhearted when his son left. He likely experienced deep pain and worry over his lost son daily. Jesus said that the father saw his son "while he was still a long way off" (Luke 15:20). It's a detail that makes it clear the father had been watching and waiting, hopeful every day for the moment his son would return. When the son arrived, the father welcomed him and threw a party.

Although the story is called the parable of the prodigal son, it has been said that it's more accurate to say it's the story of a loving father. I sometimes imagine there was a conversation before the son left home that went something like this:

Son: "I'm leaving home and there really is nothing you can do about it."

Father: "I don't want you to leave. I think you are making a very bad mistake with lifelong consequences. Nevertheless, you are an adult and I can't forbid you to leave. But know this: our home will always be open to you."

The father displayed great love and wisdom in his response. "I think you are making a bad decision and a poor choice with potentially terrible consequences. *But* I'm your father and my home is always open to you." What some parents don't understand is that you can still show love as your children suffer the natural outcome of their actions.

The son eventually did come home and his father warmly and lavishly welcomed him, but that didn't mean everything went back to the way it was. Most likely, there were still consequences. I wonder if after the welcome-home party there was another conversation that went something like this:

Father: "Son, I am so glad you are home. I have prayed for this day to arrive. You are welcome to stay, but you need to know that there are expectations and boundaries."

Son: "Dad, I am so sorry. You were right. I will do my best to live according to the way I should have been living all along. I am humbled by your loving grace."

Although Jesus doesn't spell out how the younger son

responded, I like to imagine he was willing to change and to abide by the father's lovingly set boundaries. We can learn so much about how to handle a prodigal child from this amazing parable. This father was loving yet firm. He offered grace but still expected his son to live by the family's values. My guess is that when most children return home after straying, there is much to celebrate. But don't expect it all to be easy. All of us are complicated and some of those same kids come back with addictions or habits of the heart that need work. Always be aware that some miracles take time.

WHAT TO DO WHEN YOUR ADULT CHILD MAKES REGRETTABLE CHOICES

No one said parenting a child who violates your values would be easy, but the best chance for success is when there is good communication and understanding between you. Here are some strategies that work.

Offer your adult child tough love. Tough love is a disciplined and strongly expressed boundary to promote responsible behavior and long-term change. You offer tough love when you set firm limits and enforce consequences. Tough love might mean not allowing a drug-using adult child to move back into your home without first getting help. Tough love is not being willing to bail your son out of a financial crisis one more time, even if it costs him dearly. The purpose of tough love is to stop the problematic behavior and encourage positive growth and responsibility in your adult child. Don't confuse tough love with meanness. The purpose of meanness is to be hurtful, which is the opposite of tough love. Tough love is intended to put your child on the path to healing and wholeness.

Don't bail them out. If you take on the consequences your child should be experiencing, you are robbing them of an opportunity for growth and change. Their crisis doesn't need to be your crisis. Crisis is almost always self-defined, which means that what you consider to be a crisis may not be a crisis to your child or vice versa. Don't allow your adult children to make their problems your problems.

Don't be a one-topic parent. We've talked about this principle before, but it bears repeating here. Even in the depths of heartbreak and worry, you still need to bring a balanced approach to the relationship. You don't have to give up your values to keep the relationship strong. I know a woman whose daughter had left her family's values behind and was living the life of what might be called a party girl. When the woman asked me what she should do, I said, "Since she already knows how you feel, take her to dinner once a week and talk about other things. Get to know her beyond what is breaking your heart." It worked! Eventually, her daughter turned the corner on her choices.

Don't dump your anger and frustration on your child. It's never a good idea to dump our "stuff" on them. If you need to have a conversation, and you will, make sure you aren't just unloading your feelings on them. That will only lead to resentment and further distancing. Even in the toughest times, endeavor to be their greatest cheerleader. A good friend of ours was deeply upset by her daughter's irresponsible sexual behavior and unwed pregnancy. But she was determined to maintain their relationship and found the strength to be the main support for her daughter through the pregnancy. Did she still need to vent her anger and frustration? Yes, but she did that with a trusted friend and not her daughter.

Find support for yourself. Sometimes the most difficult grief to bear is one that comes from watching our children live with self-destructive decisions, and this is something we just can't do alone. What are the replenishing and supportive relationships in your life? A healthy and supported parent has a much better chance of helping their adult child. A dad at our church brought up his son's drinking problem in a men's group he attended. It was a smart move because he needed the group's support and encouragement. He also admitted to his men's group that he had a drinking problem as well, and they helped him find a treatment center. The day after he entered treatment for his alcoholism, his son followed him into the treatment center. The dad's willingness to seek help and support was the turning point that changed his son's life. Never underestimate the power of seeking out support for yourself.

Seek professional wisdom and counsel for difficult issues. Some issues are so complex or deeply rooted that they won't be solved with a new set of boundaries and expectations. Some examples include:

- Addictions
- Trouble with the law
- Clinical depression
- Bipolar disorder
- Abuse
- Suicide attempts
- Self-injury
- Eating disorders

For issues such as these, seek professional expertise and counsel. The Bible is clear: "Where no counsel is, the people fall: but in the multitude of counsellors there is safety" (Prov. 11:14 KJV).

Relinquish your children to God's care. Releasing your children to God's care is a daily act of the will. God loves our children even more than we do. The act of relinquishment is seldom easy, but it is of utmost importance. This is the prayer I pray each day: "God, I release my children to your loving care and tender mercies." Yes, it's that simple. Every time I pray that prayer, it's a great reminder that God is in charge and I am not.

Whatever the issues causing your heart to break, remember that ultimately, the question in the heart of your adult child is, "Do you still love me?" Although it can take a great deal of discipline, we can shower our adult kids with love even when they wander off the path we had hoped for them. God's love for us is the perfect example of the unconditional love we must strive to lavish on our children. His love is unfailing and never ending, and yet he allows us to experience the natural consequences of our choices. The storyline of the entire Bible is one in which God's people rebel against him, suffer the consequences, and then are restored by God's redemptive love, which draws them back to him. That's the love we need to have for our children, a love that draws them back to us. The promise of God's story is that love *prevails*.

WHEN YOUR ADULT CHILD STRAYS FROM FAITH

My friends Jack and Jenny are leaders in the worldwide family ministry movement. Cathy and I have known them for many years and witnessed both their integrity and their excellent parenting strategies. They sacrificed financially to put their kids in a Christian school, were active in church, and lived out their Christian faith at home. Yet when their kids entered college, they quit attending church and practicing their faith. Throughout their college years, their two sons engaged in all the activities associated with a party lifestyle. When their daughter graduated from college, she moved in with her boyfriend, became pregnant, and had an abortion.

Jack and Jenny were devastated and a bit shellshocked when each of their kids chose to stray from their faith. As a result of their kids' rebellion, they even doubted their calling to help families succeed. They blamed each other. They blamed themselves. They looked for answers and tried to help, but still their young adult children strayed. Cathy and I had many conversations with Jack and Jenny during these difficult years. There were no easy answers and sometimes just more questions.

I've devoted my adult life to helping young people and their families succeed. My message has been one of spiritual commitment and hope, so when I see droves of young adults, such as Jack and Jenny's three kids, wandering away from their faith, it grieves me.

I was especially moved a few years ago when I heard Dr. Tony Campolo give a profound and personal talk titled "When Your Kid Walks Away from Faith." It was a moving message rooted in the pain of watching his son walk away from the Christian faith at age fifty. I thought he summed up the issue of adult children leaving faith well: "When young adults quit listening to the Word of God, singing about God, being stimulated in their faith with other people, and never spend time exercising their faith, the natural result is that their faith will fade. If you don't use a muscle, the muscle will atrophy. So if you don't exercise your faith, your faith will atrophy."

Tony's point was that people seldom lose their faith because of a onetime event. Instead, their faith slowly erodes because they don't use it. In that sense, faith, which is our relationship with God, is a lot like any other relationship. If we don't pay attention to a person, the relationship fades. It doesn't mean the person isn't still somehow present in our life; it just means the relationship languishes from lack of attention. Keeping faith alive and vibrant takes energy and focus and the discipline of being around others who stimulate us toward deeper faith.

I believe Tony was right—growing in faith is a discipline. "Discipline yourself for the purpose of godliness," wrote the apostle Paul to his protege Timothy (1 Tim. 4:7 NASB). Keeping faith alive requires long-term time, sacrifice, and energy. We are all either growing in faith or atrophying. There is no maintenance mode. Most people know what it takes to get in shape physically; they just don't do it. The same is true with our faith.

Children who abandon the faith are undoubtedly a source of deep pain for their parents. But even when our children have turned their backs on God, we can still choose to be filled with hope. The promise of Scripture is this: "Direct your children onto the right path, and when they are older, they will not leave it" (Prov. 22:6 NLT). If your children have walked away from the faith, anchor yourself in this promise. It is an excellent reminder that there is great hope they will eventually return to the right path. This proverb doesn't specify when they will return or how, but time, circumstances, and God's relentless love have a way of bringing the wanderers home. Until that happens, we can be faithful in prayer and in hope.

There are also a few things we can do to help our children along their faith journey. When our children reject the faith, we

The Anatomy of an Atrophied Faith

To help our adult children reclaim the faith of their youth, we must better understand what causes their loss of faith. Here are six contributing factors:

1. *Neglect.* We neglect our faith when we cease to practice spiritual disciplines, such as prayer, Bible reading, and worship. Many times, neglect starts with small compromises.

2. *Drift.* Drift is what happens when we allow events and circumstances to take us away from God. Sometimes we don't even realize we've been drifting until we look up one day and realize we are far from God.

3. *Unbelief (lack of trust).* Faith or trust in God cannot coexist with an attitude of self-reliance. Most of us are not "anti-God," but we put our trust more in our own resources than in God's love and care. But when we try to do life on our own, we quickly find out that we are finite. I've never fully understood why anyone would try to do life and relationships on their own when relying on God is so much more appealing. But where there is neglect and drift, lack of trust inevitably follows.

4. *Disobedience.* Disobedience is an act of will. "Those who accept my commandments and obey them are the ones who love me," Jesus said. "And because they love me, my Father will love them. And I will love them and reveal myself to each of them" (John 14:21 NLT). Our obedience shows that we love God and makes it

possible for Jesus to reveal himself to us. Many times, young adults distance themselves from their faith because they have chosen a lifestyle that is not God-honoring. Their disobedience makes it harder for them to see God.

5. *Insensitivity to God.* When we don't exercise our faith, we become insensitive to God and unable to experience the promptings of the Holy Spirit. Such insensitivity is a hardening of the heart. This doesn't mean we hate God, but the condition of our hearts makes it difficult to hear and respond to God's prompting and direction.

6. *Forfeiting spiritual potential.* In this final step of losing our faith, we live under the consequences of our choices and forfeit God's presence in our life. When adult children forfeit God's presence, their diminished spiritual potential is always painful for their parents.

---

can maintain a climate of openness and grace, refuse to beat ourselves up, and continue to influence them.

Maintain a climate of openness and grace. As we've already discussed, preaching and lecturing don't soften a child's heart. They seem to produce the opposite effect. Patience prevails. Your children will be attracted to the authenticity of your faith and your relationship with God. Poet Maya Angelou once wrote, "I've learned that people will forget what you said, people will forget what you did, but people will never forget how you made them feel." Make sure your children feel your love more than anything else. Consistent love and care (without enabling) is the most effective way to draw them back to faith. Our children need to know that no matter what road they travel, there's a path that leads home, and there will always be a welcome mat out for them.

Refuse to beat yourself up. You might be surprised how many of the conversations I have with parents begin with and focus on their own mistakes. "If only I had . . ." Thank God, our adult children's faith decisions are not dependent on our perfection. The last time I checked, only God is perfect. This is where the spiritual discipline of releasing our children to God and relinquishing their lives into his hands is critical. You can beat yourself up over your child's loss of faith, but it's not going to help you or them. It will only keep you focused on the past and complicate your relationship with your child. Instead, put your energy into praying for your kids and trusting God for their future. Don't give up.

Continue to influence them. Just because lectures don't work doesn't mean you can't influence your child. For example, holidays can be a good time to incorporate gentle spiritual reminders, such as an inspirational reading around the dinner table or an invitation to a special service at church.

I recently met a mom who brought her adult son and daughter-in-law to a parenting seminar at her church. They came for the seminar but ended up being impressed with the church and the church's efforts to help families succeed. Other parents periodically send a well-written Christian blog post, book, or article about a subject important to their kids. Sometimes the kids will read the material and other times they won't. As long as the articles and your intentions are not preachy, your efforts will likely be appreciated. But don't load their inbox with content without their approval.[21]

We have found that inviting our adult children who live nearby to a Sunday morning breakfast before church is a great way to get them up and moving toward attending a worship service. We have spent a lot of money on restaurant tabs and ingested some extra calories, but it seems to work for our family. Plus, we love the time together.

Remember Jack and Jenny, the couple whose three kids rebelled? After several years, their children are slowly coming back to faith. Their two sons are married with children and both want their children to be raised in the church. They now attend the same church as Jack and Jenny. They want the grandkids to be close to their grandparents. And their daughter is beginning to ask a lot more questions and even calls them from time to time to ask for prayer.

Does every story of a wayward child end happily? No, but the biblical principle still rings true: "Train up a child in the way he should go, even when he is old he will not depart from it" (Prov. 22:6 NASB). The timing and the outcome aren't in our hands, but based on my years of counseling hurting families, I can promise you that children who stray or violate your values often will return to the faith in time.

Life is complicated, and bad things sometimes do happen to good parents. As I've studied families over the years, I've often wondered, What is the formula that enables some families to thrive while others sink? I think at least part of the answer lies in two words: attitude and perspective.

Let me explain. Joni Eareckson Tada has always been a hero of mine. Now in her late sixties, Joni was paralyzed in a diving accident when she was just a teenager. All of her adult life she has suffered deep pain and has had to use a wheelchair, yet she is one of the most radiant people I have ever met. From the day I first read her story and watched a movie about her life, I have been intrigued by her amazing attitude despite her circumstances.

One afternoon about fifty years after her accident, I had the privilege of interviewing Joni for a radio broadcast. As Joni and her wonderful husband, Ken, entered the studio, I was overcome by her radiance. I scrapped my carefully prepared interview questions and simply asked, "Joni, how do you manage to be so radiant in the midst of your pain and suffering?"

She looked at me thoughtfully for a few moments and then she smiled and said, "Jim, every day I find reasons amid my pain to be thankful for life. The Bible says, 'Give thanks in everything you do,' and I guess that has become the reflex reaction for my life."

The phrase "reflex reaction" stood out to me. Even in her toughest times, Joni made thankfulness and gratitude a habit of her heart. Her difficult circumstance had not changed—she was not miraculously healed—but her attitude was one of deep joy because she chose to be thankful. Not only was Joni's attitude amazing but so was her perspective. I would have looked at a diving accident as a horrible event in my life. Joni's perspective was that the diving accident, as awful as it was, gave her the opportunity to share good news with millions of people and to come alongside others who needed the hope she was uniquely equipped to give.

After the interview, I reflected on her words for the rest of that day. Cathy and I had been going through a rough spot with one of our daughters. Joni's words didn't solve the issue, but she gave us perspective that even during what we considered to be

a hard time, we could find joy in the journey by making gratitude our reflex reaction.

It's painful when a child violates our values. It almost
always causes us to doubt our ability to parent, and to wonder
what went wrong. But even when we can't change our circumstances, the attitude and perspective we choose can and will
make the difference. So let's follow Joni's example and take a
victory any way we can.

If you are anything like me, you want your kids to thrive
almost more than anything else in life. I can't end your pain,
but this I do know from experience: God promises to walk with
you through the shadow of death and back. Continue to pray
for your kids. I'm so glad that when we pray for our kids and
our family, the power of prayer does not come from our words
but from the one who hears our words and loves us with an
unfailing love.

CHAPTER 7

THE HIGH COST
OF MONEY

PRINCIPLE 7: FINANCIAL INDEPENDENCE
AND RESPONSIBILITY IS THE GOAL

Dear Dad,

$chool i$ really great. I am making lot$ of friend$ and $tudying very hard. With all my $tuff, I $imply can't think of anything I need. $o if you would like, you can ju$t $end me a card, a$ I would love to hear from you.

Love,

Your $on

Dear Son,

I kNOw that astroNOmy, ecoNOmics, and OceaNOgraphy are eNOugh to keep even an hoNOr student busy. Do NOt forget that the pursuit of kNOwledge is a NOble task, and that you can never study eNOugh.

Love,

Dad

┼·┼·┼

A young man asked an older, wiser man, "What will it take for me to become financially healthy and responsible?"

The older man, who was a successful businessperson, smiled and said, "Two words: good decisions."

"But how do I learn to make good decisions?" the young man asked.

The older man said, "One word: experience."

The young man pressed for details. "But how do I gain experience?"

The older man replied, "Two words: bad decisions."

I've always liked this story because it succinctly describes how most of us learn to handle money. As it is in other areas of life, parents who make a habit of bailing their adult children out of bad financial choices only stifle their children's ability to develop healthy financial muscles and to become responsible and independent with their finances.

If you help your adult kids financially, know this: you are not alone. More than 75 percent of parents give their adult children some form of financial help in one season or another. And at the same time, money problems can be a major source of concern and conflict between parents and adult children.

According to the groundbreaking research of Jeffrey Arnett in "The Clark University Poll of Parents of Emerging Adults," money problems rank number one as the most common worry or concern parents have about their adult children. It ranked higher than choosing the wrong romantic partner, lack of work, and educational progress.[22]

There is a high cost for ignoring the money dynamic in our relationships with our children. If we don't discuss money openly with them, it won't go away; it will only become more complicated. There will be hurt feelings and misunderstandings and potentially even a breakdown in the relationship. Money, perhaps more than any other issue, has the power to drive a wedge between us if we don't talk about it with our children.

Karen and Eric came to my office for a conversation about what they called "the money pit." Most people use that term for a high-maintenance home, car, or boat, but they used it for their twenty-six-year-old son, Lance. Their son was in the failure-to-launch stage of emerging adulthood. He was still on his parents' payroll, and there was little reason to hope he would move to the next stage of responsible adulthood anytime soon.

The more they talked and pointed to Lance's lack of financial responsibility, the more I sensed that the problem wasn't entirely with their son. They kept calling him the money pit, but I started to believe they were contributing more to the problem than just money. Sure, their son was not being responsible, but it also became increasingly clear that they were enabling his irresponsible behavior.

"Why is it that you continue to pay your son's way? Does he have a disability or some other reason he's not able to support himself?" I asked.

THE HIGH COST OF MONEY

"No," Eric said. "Lance has never been a high achiever, but he doesn't have a disability or learning issue that's holding him back. He's fully capable of working."

Then out of the blue, Karen began to cry. "I'm afraid if we don't keep taking care of him he will become homeless or start taking drugs or make a horrible decision with a girl!" she blurted.

Ah, now we were getting somewhere. Karen's fear was real and legitimate to a degree. I didn't question her desire to protect her son from bad choices. But Karen and Eric's financial coddling wasn't necessary. Instead of fostering independence and financial responsibility, they were reinforcing Lance's dependency. Despite their love and best intentions, they had an entitled man-child on their hands. If things kept going the same way, it wouldn't end well for anyone.

Back to Karen's fears. Her fears were normal for any loving parent. No parent wants to see a child end up homeless, make unwise decisions, or lead a negative lifestyle. But this is where parents must face their fears and decide what is best for their child in the long run. If Karen and Eric were going to help Lance become a responsible adult, they needed to implement a tough-love money policy. The question they had to ask themselves wasn't whether their son would be able to find his next meal or get a job, it was, "Will providing more money help our son to become self-sufficient, or will it prolong his dependence on us?" The only healthy response to a situation like Karen and Eric's was to stop pouring cash into the money pit. They had to quit bailing him out.

Your adult children may not be irresponsible with their finances, but if you are still paying for their cell phone and other bills, that's enabling. Quite often, love means saying no, even if you can afford to say yes. Saying no and stopping the flow of money to your adult children may be the most effective thing you can do to help them take their next step toward financial responsibility. Keep in mind that the first step in any healing process is often the most painful. I've always told my kids that "before freedom often comes pain," and that's why we must keep the great goal of financial independence in mind. Things will get better!

KEEP THE GOAL IN MIND: FINANCIAL RESPONSIBILITY AND INDEPENDENCE

The old saying "Give a man a fish, feed him for a day; teach a man to fish, feed him for a lifetime" works in helping adult children become responsible with finances. We do this when we teach our children foundational principles about money and then help them develop a simple and practical plan. Unfortunately, most of us spent little to no time creating a roadmap to successful financial responsibility when our kids were younger. As parents of children and teenagers, we were just trying to make it through one day to the next. But all is not lost. If our adult kids are dependent on us financially, we still have the leverage we need to help them practice responsible stewardship. Doing so will not only enable our children to become financially accountable adults but also help them in their marriage and family relationships down the road.

Here are two things every parent of a financially dependent adult child can do: develop a clear exit strategy and foster independence.

Develop a Clear Exit Strategy

A clear exit strategy is a plan to end parental financial aid. It means your child is clear about what you will and will not pay for when your financial support ends. In our family, we made sure our girls knew what we would pay for college and weddings long before there was a college admission letter or a wedding. It's not fair to pull the financial rug out from under your adult child if you haven't first discussed what they can expect from you.

Kathy and Eric decided to create a simple plan together with Lance. Deep down, Lance wanted to grow up and become responsible with his finances and his life. Since people support what they help create, the family ended up making an appointment with a family friend who was a financial planner. Together, they came up with a plan they could all agree on. Later, Kathy and Eric told me there were a few slipups along the way, but now everyone was feeling better about the situation and Lance was successfully out on his own. Without a plan, that wouldn't have happened.

Foster Independence

Our friends Rebecca and Michael took seriously the job of teaching their kids financial responsibility. At age sixteen, each of their three children were expected to sit with Mom and Dad to learn the discipline of paying family bills, to balance the checkbook, and to work with their parents on preparing tax returns. They were also allowed to provide some input on the family's giving and investment strategies. It may sound a little crazy, but it worked. All three of their kids are now financially independent and responsible adults. Obviously, the kids didn't make decisions about family finances on their own, and it was undoubtedly more time consuming to allow the kids to help with the bills, the checkbook, and the taxes, but the mentoring the kids received was well worth the time and effort.

In our family, we gave the kids an allowance associated with their weekly chores. When they reached a certain age, we also gave them larger sums of money to buy school clothes on their own. Having all daughters, we had some dramatic learning experiences and a few disastrous choices in the clothes, makeup, and hairstyling departments, but they all survived. Their allowance ended after college. Another couple we know met with their children as they entered college and explained, "Here's what we will do financially for you through your four years of college. After college, we will continue to help for three months, and then we are cutting the strings." Whatever decisions you make, just be sure both you and your kids have clarity.

Many parents have to learn the hard way not to allow their children to become money pits. One financially well-off couple met with me because their son was addicted to heroin. "How does he pay for it?" I asked. It turned out he had a large monthly allowance. The father looked at his wife and said, "I guess we pay for it!" Remember, self-sufficiency is the goal. If your child is making poor choices, don't support those choices financially.

TEACH AND TRAIN YOUR KIDS ABOUT HEALTHY FINANCIAL PRINCIPLES

A much better gift than handing money to your adult children is teaching them to be good stewards of their own money. It's a gift most parents fail to give. I've worked with hundreds of young couples in premarital counseling and education through our *Getting Ready for Marriage* book, workbook, and online app *(www.gettingreadyformarriage.com)*. When asked whether they received much help or training in financial responsibility from their parents, few tell me their parents took this area of training seriously. Some say their parents modeled good behavior, but not one has said that they received the guidance they needed.

Let's face it: money is a problem for most families. Most don't believe they have enough, and perhaps a majority are caught up in too much debt or other financial problems. More often than not, at least a portion of those troubles are because of poor decisions and planning. All the studies I know of clearly demonstrate that families, whether they are rich, poor, or somewhere in the middle, are happier and more satisfied with life if they handle their money in a healthy way.

Although I am by no means a financial expert, Cathy and I decided to teach our kids about responsible stewardship as part of our family mentoring. We have been greatly influenced by the late Ron Blue, who was a wonderful financial planner. Here is what Ron taught us about biblical money management and stewardship principles:

- God owns it all.
- There is a trade-off between time and effort and money and rewards.
- There is no such thing as an "independent financial decision."
- Delayed gratification is the key to financial maturity.[23]

Drawing on these excellent words of advice, here are the six money management principles we taught our kids.

1. Spend less than you make. The first time I spoke to an audience of parents on the topic of teaching financial principles to their kids, I added the word "duh" at the end of this principle: "Spend less than you make. Duh." I added it for comic relief, but no one laughed. As we sat in discussion groups after the talk, parents kept coming back to the need not only to teach this principle to their children but also to live it out themselves. With the collective personal debt of Americans now topping $13 trillion,[24] and the fact that more than 57 percent of Americans do not have even a thousand dollars in savings to tap for emergency purposes,[25] the issue of debt is a big deal. Spending less than you make may sound simplistic, but it is a major part of financial responsibility.

2. Debt is slavery. Too many emerging adults have a mindset of "spend today with credit and pay it off over time." Bad idea. Incurring credit card interest and debt is poor stewardship, and we've all heard the painful stories of young adults whose substantial student loan debt hobbled them financially for a decade or more after graduation. Jordan, the son of a friend of mine, signed up for a credit card his first year of college and immediately went out and bought a thousand-dollar bike. He had a part-time job and his goal was to pay it off in four years. What he failed to realize was that with interest, the cost of the bike would double during those four years. And it wasn't like he had to have the bike to get to work or school. He told his parents he had ridden the bike only a few times since he bought it. Now he has a two-thousand-dollar bike gathering dust in the garage, and he is still making payments on it every month. Debt is slavery.

3. Delayed gratification is the answer. Just for fun, I asked our two-year-old grandson, James, if he wanted an ice cream cone or a fifty-dollar bill to be put in a savings account. He looked at me as if I were crazy and said, "I want ice cream." Since he's a toddler with no real concept of money, I expected him to say that. Unfortunately, this "I want it now" mentality doesn't stop with toddlerhood; it's pervasive among young and old in our society. Little James has an excuse—he's two! But there's no excuse for the rest of us.

You are the model your kids need. When you delay gratification of things you want, you help your kids understand the important difference between needs and wants. You can also teach your kids the power of compounding interest. Compounding interest essentially means the "interest on interest" and is the reason so many investors are successful. When we put off gratification today by investing for tomorrow, the returns can be significant. I was just telling one of my adult daughters that if someone had invested five thousand dollars in Amazon stock in 1997, twenty years later that investment would be worth more than a million dollars.

4. Give 10 percent, save 10 percent. We tried to teach our kids that we had never met a person with major financial problems who consistently gave 10 percent of their income to charity and put 10 percent in savings. This may be an oversimplification, but my experience is that givers and savers do much better over time.

5. A budget is a must. There have been several studies looking at the finances of people who are financially successful. The people themselves were diverse, but they had one thing in common: they lived within a budget. One of the greatest gifts you can give your children is the ability to create and follow a budget. A budget is the roadmap to help your children know how they are doing financially and whether they are staying on track. When I do premarital counseling, I find that most young couples have never used a budget or been taught by their parents how to create one. One of the sessions I do with each couple is on finances, and I tell them I won't meet with them unless they bring in a budget. Helping your kids create a budget is a great opportunity for you to mentor your kids now and for the future.

6. Don't be afraid to talk about money, especially when it hasn't been handled well. John and Shelly told their daughter Macy they would pay for her college education on the condition that she maintained a B average. One semester, Macy put more energy into her sorority life than her studies. She took a few road trips, failed to complete some assignments, and never caught up. Her grades that semester fell well below the required B average.

When her parents found out, they sat down with Macy and said, "We understand. Things like this can happen in college. Nevertheless, we were clear about the fact that if you didn't do what you are easily capable of by maintaining a B average, we would temporarily stop the flow of money for school."

Macy cried and begged for a second chance. I like the solution John and Shelly came up with. They told their daughter she would have to figure out how to pay for the next semester on her own. But if she maintained a B average, they would repay her after the semester was over. Macy didn't love the setup, but she scrambled to get a loan and did the work to maintain that B average. Macy learned a valuable lesson about financial responsibility, and her parents were able to keep their relationship with her intact because they weren't afraid to talk about money.

I know other parents who had the capacity to provide their young marrieds with a down payment for a home. Instead, they sat down with them and said they would match their savings dollar for dollar. Three years later, the young couple came back to them and took advantage of their generosity. Again, talking about money set clear expectations, promoted financial independence in their kids, and kept the relationship strong.

If your adult child is willing, stay on as their financial coach and mentor. Even if you don't have a perfect financial record yourself, be willing to learn together. I know a couple who sponsored their adult married children to attend a Financial Peace University series at their church. They offered to babysit the grandkids, but since the church was offering free babysitting, their married kids invited them to join them. Together, they learned some biblical financial principles that helped both couples to strengthen their financial situation. Their relationship became much more open about financial responsibility and allowed the parents to speak into their kids' lives as mentors on principles of healthy stewardship. If we can teach our adult children that "the best things in life are not things," we have done a good job.

ADULT CHILDREN AND YOUR ESTATE PLAN

Even if you don't have tons of money to leave to your children, it's important to think about your estate in terms of legacy and impact. No matter how much you have, don't leave your kids in the dark as one couple did. With a net worth of $300 million, this couple was extraordinarily wealthy. They were also committed and generous Christian philanthropists. It was only after both parents had died that their children discovered that the entire estate had been left to a charitable foundation. The children were shocked and dismayed that they were left nothing. Their parents had every right to leave their money to whomever they wanted, but they should have communicated their intentions to their adult children. The unfortunate outcome was that the children fought among themselves, sued the foundation, and caused a great deal of trouble and anguish for everyone involved.

Here's the lesson I learned from this situation: whether or not you have money to leave for inheritance, communicate your plans with your kids. Put it in writing by leaving a will or a living trust. If you don't have a will or living trust, put this book down and take care of it today. It's that important. Leaving it up to your kids to sort out your estate after you're gone is a selfish act. Make your estate a "no surprise" estate.

Along the same lines, communicate your preferences and plans for end-of-life health issues. Few families like to talk about it, but it's so helpful for your loved ones. When my father died, we all knew exactly what he wanted. He made those decisions so much easier for us. As the executor of his living trust, I had talked with him about everything and there were no surprises. Talking things through and honoring my father's wishes was a healthy way to work through the grief of my loss.

IT'S THE PAIN OF DISCIPLINE OR THE PAIN OF REGRET

One of the best things you can do for your adult children is to teach them the lesson of good financial stewardship. An unhealthy relationship with money brings regret, misunderstanding, and

An Open Letter to Parents Who
Financially Support Adult Children

Peter Dunn is a sought-after speaker and columnist for *USA Today*. He had some great advice for parents of adult children in a column he wrote titled "An Open Letter to Parents Who Financially Support Adult Children." Here is an excerpt:

> I write to you not from a place of judgment, but instead I address you based on an immense body of work that has brought me great clarity. The financial support you are offering your adult children is toxic. You are hurting them, you are hurting yourself, and until you realize it's not money that they need, everyone involved will feel the pain.
>
> Think back to when you taught your child to ride her bicycle without training wheels. Who was more scared? The idea of letting go of a toddler rocketing across concrete with little protection is terrifying. If you let go, she will fall—she will bleed. If you don't, she will never learn to ride the most elementary transportation device since the invention of feet. Once you let go, and she falls and bleeds, she will quickly learn that balance and control equal the absence of pain. At that moment, everyone moves on with their life.
>
> Assuming your now twenty- or thirty-something can ride their bike without training wheels, what was the primary element in their initial bike-riding achievement? It was your willingness to remove yourself from the situation, with the disturbing knowledge your absence would result in pain.

sometimes broken relationships. Children won't just drift into a healthy relationship with money; making good financial decisions requires discipline and a plan. Money is not going to bring happiness, but living within your means with good stewardship can keep both you and your kids from all kinds of regret.

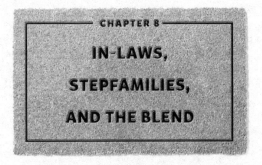

CHAPTER 8

IN-LAWS, STEPFAMILIES, AND THE BLEND

PRINCIPLE 8: WEAR BEIGE AND KEEP YOUR MOUTH SHUT

✦•✦

"The first forty years of parenting are always the hardest!"

☧·☧·☧

A woman I know was asked at her son's wedding, "What is the responsibility of the mother of the groom?" She smiled and said, "Wear beige and keep your mouth shut." She got a chuckle, but it was great advice, especially when it comes to relationships with in-laws.

Many comedians like to do a bit on in-laws, especially a mother-in-law. I must admit I have done my share of laughing at those jokes. The reason so many comedians take on the in-law routine is because the in-law stereotypes are based on realities most people can relate to. Some in-laws *do* meddle. When it comes to dealing with in-laws, stepfamilies, and the blend, the wisecrack wisdom of "wear beige and keep your mouth shut" is a much more effective strategy than meddling. Here's my short take on navigating a successful relationship with an in-law or an in-law-to-be:

- Don't criticize the in-law.
- Don't criticize the in-law's parenting.
- Don't criticize the in-law's treatment of your son or daughter.
- Don't criticize *anything* about the in-law.

If I might be so blunt, it's not about you; it's about them. You don't have to like them. You don't have to agree with them. Your job is to honor your child by honoring your in-law because they chose your in-law and you didn't.

Susan and Matt confided in me that their new daughter-in-law was not the type of person they had hoped their son would marry. She was brash, bossy, opinionated, and a bit narcissistic. They also felt she was keeping their son away from the family. While Matt wanted to confront the couple, Susan was nervous that a confrontation would push her new daughter-in-law and son away. They asked me what I thought. Although I do believe that gentle confrontations can work, I wasn't sure that was the best strategy in this case.

"It seems like she is a bit rough around the edges," I said. "I'd shower her with kindness and pray for a transformation. It doesn't sound like she has a vendetta against you as much as this is her personality with everyone. What if you took on the task of nixing any negativity toward her or your son? Be the people in their lives who support their marriage. Be the safe in-laws to whom they will be drawn, rather than the ones causing tension. Lower your expectations for a while and support them whenever and however you can."

Susan also shared she was struggling over the loss of closeness with her son. Before his marriage, the son and his mother had been close. Now, not so much. "Your access to your son and future grandkids is through your daughter-in-law," I said. "So it's back to supporting her in any way you can. Without being intrusive, offer to babysit anytime she needs a break and it works with your schedule. Go out of your way to bring her a small gift or write an affirming card. You'd do it for a friend, so why not for your daughter-in-law, who can become your friend? When you honor her, you are honoring your son. Be the person they want to spend time with because you are investing in their lives. Then sit back and watch the relationship change."

I know my advice to Susan might sound like an oversimplification because life and relationships can get complicated—even good, well-intentioned people can make mistakes when hurt feelings get the best of them. But for those in Susan's situation, the decision to support the marriage of your grown kids can help keep it from being unnecessarily complicated. Stay away from disputes with your kid's spouse on *anything*. You just can't take it personally.

WHAT IF YOU DON'T LIKE THEM?

Sometimes people tell me they just don't like the person their adult child is dating or has married. I get it. But unless the situation is abusive or destructive, it's better to focus on learning to like them than to focus on what you don't like about them.

One mom I know changed a relationship with her daughter-in-law through small gifts. Her daughter-in-law had a shell that was difficult to penetrate. She didn't have much of a filter and would say hurtful words to her mother-in-law and talk negatively about her son. She was simply a negative and draining person. One day when the mom was at Starbucks, she realized that her daughter-in-law loved Starbucks, but the young couple was on a pretty tight budget. So the mom bought her a ten-dollar gift card. Next door was a candy store that sold chocolate-dipped strawberries, and she purchased two. On her way home, she stopped by her son and daughter-in-law's apartment with the gift card, strawberries, and a short note. The daughter-in-law loved the gesture. From that time on, it became a weekly ritual. Eventually, the daughter-in-law reached out and asked to get together for coffee. One year later, they are best friends. Of course, this wonderful ending isn't always the case, but the point is clear: reach out in love, even if you don't start off liking them.

Carly and David pulled me aside at one of our *Doing Life with Your Adult Child* seminars. They told me they had taken an instant disliking to their daughter's husband and made both subtle and not-so-subtle comments to their daughter about him before the wedding. Their daughter went ahead and married, and now they were the proud grandparents of three children and still not too crazy about their son-in-law. But their story was a good one.

They decided against complaining about the son-in-law to their daughter. Even when she made negative comments (with which they agreed), they kept quiet. They just listened. Their philosophy was, "He's your husband and we will stay out of the fray." When grandchildren entered the picture, the son-in-law routinely limited their access to the grandkids and the hurts deepened. When Carly and David asked to stop by, he would say, "Not today—we are really busy." They waited for more access with wounded hearts. They offered to babysit. They bought gifts. They didn't miss any occasion to celebrate together. Slowly but surely, access was granted. Babysitters were needed, and they got their time. They were smart enough to wait it out and keep their mouths shut, and eventually things changed.

When I asked them how the breakthrough happened, they

said, "We decided to become the fun grandparents and fun in-laws. This meant our grandkids started asking for us. We tried to create family fun as a vital part of our family culture." When I asked if they liked their son-in-law any better, they said, "When we lowered our expectations and accepted him for who he is, things got better. We want to do everything we can to help them succeed as a family."

While some may chafe at the thought, the idea of wearing beige and keeping your mouth shut really is wise counsel and the most effective way to deal with in-laws, stepfamilies, and blended family relationships. If you get it wrong, the consequences may be far more painful than the effort required to act with restraint. That's what happened with Marie, who was vocal in expressing her dislike of her daughter Cally's choice in a husband.

From the beginning, Marie's relationship with her son-in-law was strained and the relationship with her daughter was complicated as a result. Before Cally married her husband, Marie saw what she considered to be red flags in the relationship, and she wasn't shy about telling everyone she knew what she thought of him. Cally married him anyway. They had a baby. The marriage was rocky at best. When Cally separated from her husband, Marie didn't let a day go by without giving her daughter a piece of her mind about her lousy, good-for-nothing husband. As much as Cally tried to distance herself from her mother's negativity, it was still a regular part of life. Then one day, Cally told her mom that because of the baby, she and her husband were going to try to reconcile. That same week, while in the middle of a fight with her husband, Cally told her husband what Marie thought of him. Later, the husband called

Marie and told her she was no longer welcome in their home. He cut off access to her daughter and grandson. It was only in hindsight that Marie recognized she shouldn't have unleashed her anger and concerns on her daughter. It had cost her the relationship.

FIVE TIPS TO NAVIGATE THE RELATIONSHIP

As we work through the five tips that follow, keep in mind the principle of this chapter, "wear beige and keep your mouth shut." It effectively summarizes the best approach to navigating and improving a relationship with an in-law. One woman told me, "I'm surprised my tongue doesn't have scars from the number of times I've had to bite it!" When you keep in front of you the goal of having a good and loving relationship, most other things won't matter. Before I react or speak to an in-law, I like to ask myself this question: "Will what I am about to say or do improve the relationship?" Don't make it about you; make it about the health of the relationship. The following tips will help.

1. Don't make your child choose between you and their new family. One of the many mistakes Marie made in expressing her disapproval was forcing her daughter to choose between her and her husband. This shouldn't have happened. One young adult said, "Too often, my mom was the wedge between my husband and me, so the only answer was to distance myself from my mom." You may not approve of your son or daughter's spouse, but you can still show love to your in-law for your adult child's sake.

2. Don't complain. At least 25 percent of parents end up

living with their children sometime during their aging years. Complaints and criticisms may force your children to choose between you or themselves, and invariably you will be the one aced out of the relationship. Constant complaints or criticisms of your in-law will jeopardize your relationship. Be careful with your comments and be quick to overlook minor offenses or slights. Things have a way of working out if you haven't offended them with complaining.

3. Don't stub your toe on old family issues. Put the past where it belongs—in the past. Mend the relationship if it needs mending. Too many families are still at war over an offense that happened years before. Be the first one to put negative family patterns on the shelf. When you take the lead, your children or other family members will typically follow, and even if they don't, you are still better off. A sincere apology, even if rejected, is the mature and right way to handle anything you might need to own up to. If you were the offended party, be quick to overlook any minor or irritating offenses. Does it really matter? Most things don't.

4. Offer support. If your adult child's marriage is struggling or fails, provide support. If you live in the area and your grandkids need a babysitter, be the first to offer. You honor your child and your in-law when you are their chief cheerleader. Be there for them.

When Janet and Mark's thirty-five-year-old daughter went through a messy divorce, they welcomed her home along with the three grandkids. There really wasn't enough space for all of them in the home, and it was chaotic at times, but the gift of support they provided their daughter and grandkids became a catalyst for healing from a painful divorce and helped their daughter to get back on her feet. Janet and Mark's support was strategic—they traded their own short-term comfort for a long-term legacy. They remained close to the grandchildren. They didn't bad-mouth the ex. As they took the high road of support, they turned to safe friends—not their daughter—to help them deal with their own grief and loss.

5. Negotiate holidays for a win-win. When we were first married, Cathy and I always struggled with where to spend the holidays. We wanted to celebrate with our extended families, but they didn't live close. Because we had children, we also wanted to create our own family holiday traditions. There were times when juggling the holidays felt like more of a burden than a joy. We decided that as our adult children got married, we would never pressure them to participate in our celebrations, and we would try to make their holidays as easy as possible.

The first year after our oldest daughter was married, she let us know that she would be having Thanksgiving with her in-laws. Frankly, even though we had decided not to make holidays stressful, it was a bit difficult. Then I had an idea. "How about celebrating Thanksgiving with our family on the Sunday before?" I asked. "That way you can connect with both families." She jumped at the chance for a family gathering on a separate day. We had a great time, and then on the day of Thanksgiving, we drove out to Palm Springs for a few days with one of our other daughters. It became a win-win. With some families who don't live in the area, it can't be that simple, but with an attitude of adaptability and trying to take the pressure off the kids, you most likely will get a better chance to celebrate together around a holiday. Be the in-laws who make it easy for them.

NEGOTIATING YOUR STEPFAMILY
AND BLENDED FAMILY

With the divorce rate still near the 50 percent range, stepfamilies and blended families are becoming more and more the norm. One of your tasks as a parent is to find your place in the complexity of a blended family. When things don't go perfectly, you can't take it personally. Blending a family, dealing with an ex, and navigating others' family traditions as well as dysfunctions are all part of the mix.

It goes without saying that the blending of families is a difficult undertaking. First, a couple gets a divorce or experiences the death of a spouse. After the divorce or death, there is a time of grief and loneliness. Then a new person comes along and two people fall in love. At the same time, there are existing relationships from the previous marriage. Falling in love is easy, but blending all those complex relationships is difficult. Don't expect immediate compatibility with everyone. Perhaps you have also been through a divorce or death. If that is the case, you may have a better handle on how to deal with a stepfamily and blended family. Here are a few dos of step-grandparenting.

Do:

- Win over the step-grandchildren by offering kindness and support. Work on your likability factor. Offer warmth and positivity.
- Be aware that there are always loyalty issues in a blended family, so steer clear of controversy with other family members.

- Build up a great relationship with the biological parent. It's the key to access to the step-grandkids.
- Be present in their lives whenever you can. If they live in the area, be present at their Little League games and dance recitals. Be the one to bring the flowers or buy the burgers.
- Accept your step-grandchildren as fully your own. The sooner they feel your love and acceptance, the better.
- Be generous with fun and thoughtful gifts.
- Take your cues from the biological parent.
- Allow the biological parent to discipline the kids. You are not the one to discipline.
- Assume that they might not call you Grandma or Grandpa. If they do, great; but if they don't, does it really matter? Not really. Over time, you can come up with a unique name together.
- Set boundaries, be honest, demonstrate compassion, and if you are married, remain as united as possible.
- Be sensitive to the fact that step-grandkids may need space to figure out their role in the new family culture.

I love the somewhat corny story of the visiting pastor who attended a men's breakfast in the middle of a rural farming area of the country. The group had asked an older farmer decked out in ancient overalls to say grace for the morning breakfast. "Lord, I hate buttermilk," the farmer began. The visiting pastor opened one eye to glance at the farmer and wondered where this was going. The farmer loudly proclaimed, "Lord, I hate lard." Now the pastor was growing concerned. Without missing a beat, the farmer continued, "And Lord, you know I don't care much for raw white flour." The pastor once again opened an eye to glance around the room and saw that he wasn't the only one who was beginning to feel uncomfortable. Then the farmer added, "But Lord, when you mix 'em all together and bake 'em, I do love warm, fresh biscuits. So Lord, when things come up we don't like, when life gets hard, when we just don't understand what you are sayin' to us, help us to just relax and wait till you're done mixin'. And probably it will be somethin' even better than biscuits. Amen."

Within that silly prayer there is great wisdom for all when it comes to adult children and our often complicated family situations. To adapt a few words from the wonderful Disney movie *Lilo and Stitch*, "This is my family. It's little and sometimes broken, but still good. Yeah, still good."

CHAPTER 9

IT'S PARTY TIME WITH THE GRANDKIDS

PRINCIPLE 9: BEING A GRANDPARENT MAY BE YOUR GREATEST LEGACY

✦•✦

"My grandkids think I am the oldest person in the world, and after watching them for a weekend while their parents were away, I think they are right."

⊹⊹⊹

You would have liked my grandma Nene. She was a larger than life woman who wore funny shoes and a housedress, and let her hair go prematurely gray. She never colored it. She was a character. She worked most of her adult life at the shipyards in Long Beach, California, and although I saw her get angry only a few times, she could curse like a sailor. Now, I know a lot of people in naval professions who do not cuss, but my Nene was not one of them. She wasn't an imposing or striking woman—I like to say she was four feet seven inches by four feet seven inches—but that didn't matter at all. My Nene meant the world to me.

She came to our house every Saturday to help my mom with housework and to iron everything (including underwear!). She set the most positive atmosphere in her home and ours that I have ever experienced. She cheered us on with no strings attached. She dished out dollar bills, candy, and love. My friends adored her, and as I got older, we would all go to Nene's house near the beach for much of the summer. We had more fun and laughs with her than we did anywhere else. She also put us to work, but we never minded because when you were in Nene's presence, it was party time. She could create a party out of anything.

My mom was a lot like her mother. As I've already mentioned, my kids considered her the party-time grandma. She had a drawer she kept stocked with cheap little gifts for my kids. They called them treasures. (I called them junk.) Mom knew how to make people feel welcomed and loved. She was everyone's favorite grandma.

I don't think I can match these two all-star grandparents, but not a day goes by that I don't think about trying to be the party-time grandpa for my grandkids. If you and I were having coffee together, I can guarantee you that I already would have shown you several photos of my grandkids and most likely a video or two of my fun-loving two-year-old grandson, James, hitting a golf ball. My new go-to video clip is of James sitting on the potty and telling me to get out of the bathroom. "Let me do my business!" he declares loudly. I promise I'll quit showing it to people when he gets older and would be mortified, but I will always relish these small, silly moments that bring humor and joy to my life as a grandpa.

There is perhaps no greater calling in the world than to leave a legacy of love for your grandchildren. What's great about grandparenting is that you can "stay out of the weeds" of everyday parenting and focus on the truly important issues. The Bible says, "Children's children are a crown to the aged" (Prov. 17:6). Even though, like me, you may not yet feel aged, the image of a crown conveys royalty and privilege. I now look at my calling as a grandparent as a royal, high calling from God, a sacred calling.

If you had a rough time with your kids, then grandparenting can give you a fresh start and a new purpose. Jesus' disciples once asked him, "Who is greatest in the Kingdom of Heaven?"

(Matt. 18:1 NLT). His answer certainly startled them. Instead of pointing to a famous Jewish rabbi or a powerful Roman leader, he pointed out a child. Authors Tim and Darcy Kimmel write, "When a child is born, he is the closest he will ever be to the image of God."[26] Jesus also said, "Let the little children come to me, and do not hinder them, for the kingdom of heaven belongs to such as these" (Matt. 19:14). As a grandparent, you have the privilege of furthering God's kingdom through the legacy you leave with your grandchildren. An incredible calling indeed!

As I mentioned previously, I've done several focus groups and spoken to thousands of parents about doing life with adult children. Sometimes the atmosphere is tense and emotional because of tough situations, but every time I mention grandchildren—in a casual conversation, onstage, or in a focus group—the mood immediately changes to one of great joy. Yet there are some grandparents who choose to miss out on one of God's greatest blessings. I will never understand how a grandparent can say things like, "I don't have time to watch the grandkids or attend their events. I worked hard and now I need my freedom." Even when grandparents quit working, they don't need to put their lives on cruise control, retire to the rocker, and watch old golf tournament reruns when they have grandchildren to influence and love. They are missing out on the joy grandkids bring.

My friends Reggie Joiner and Kristen Ivy of the Orange Rethink Group created a most incredible movement called It's Just a Phase . . . Don't Miss It. The premise is that from the time a child is born to the time they are launched into adulthood at eighteen, you have 936 weeks with them. That's it. We must make each day, each week, each month, and each year count.

I have a Parent Cue app[27] on my phone that counts the weeks and helps me understand some of the developmental stages my grandchildren are living through at any point on their journey to adulthood. Here's an amazing thought: Given that people are living longer today than any previous generation, you could possibly spend two decades of your life helping your grandchildren launch into responsible adulthood. During those two decades, you can help your grandkids experience a level of love, security, and stability that few others in their lives can provide. You can offer them a wonderful representation of the generations of your family. Grandparenting experts Tim and Darcy Kimmel say it this way: "We are the link to the past, the anchor to the present, and the bridge to the future."[28]

WALKING IN YOUR FOOTPRINTS

When I was young, my mom and dad would take me to the beach. I loved playing in the sand and swimming with my dad. One of the games I played without telling my dad was walking inside the impressions of his footprints in the sand. Reflecting on that memory, I see it as a metaphor for what we provide as both parents and grandparents. There is a biblical proverb that says, "A good person leaves an inheritance for their children's children" (Prov. 13:22). Yes, that applies to finances, but perhaps even more, it applies to the spiritual legacy we leave that will last long after we are in our eternal home. Our footprints are the clear tracks for our grandchildren to follow. Our legacy has great eternal value.

Another biblical truth I hold dear to my heart is Psalm 71:17–18. Here is how I paraphrase it: "You have done so much for me, God, and even when I am old and gray, I will continue to declare your power and love to the next generations." The Bible is clear that each of us leaves a legacy and an impact that lasts from generation to generation. You don't have to leave your grandkids a great amount of wealth as an inheritance; your spiritual leadership and guidance are of far greater value.

Recently, I was talking with a woman after giving a speech at a family conference. I asked her who had been significant in her spiritual development as a child. Without a moment's hesitation she said, "My grandma. She was the one who prayed for me every day. She would pick me up for church every Sunday morning and then take me out for lunch. My parents weren't much on going to church, but that didn't stop my grandma from always making it a priority. Today, I'm raising my children with much more of my grandmother's style of faith than my parents'. My kids didn't get to know my grandma, but I hope through me, they are experiencing her love and faithfulness." I was deeply inspired by this story of a grandmother's faith now influencing the great-grandchildren she never even met. My frequent and silent prayer is that I will finish strong and be faithful to my calling as a grandparent. "For the LORD is good and his love endures forever; his faithfulness continues through all generations" (Ps. 100:5).

PRACTICAL IDEAS FOR INFLUENCING YOUR GRANDKIDS

There are so many practical ways to influence your grandkids. Here are several ideas to get you started:

Be present. Be fun. Be generous. Your presence matters. I

call this "the power of being there." Even if your grandkids are scattered around the country, you can be their digital positive influence. Keep in touch regularly. I know a grandpa who sends his ten-year-old grandson a joke a day. Be a generous grandparent with thoughtful gifts and generous acts of kindness as well. If you live nearby, don't miss many games or recitals. Be the chief babysitter when they are little. Your fun and generous presence matters. Your grandkids will not refuse fun.

When our daughter Christy told us she was pregnant with our first grandchild, my wife, Cathy, had a decision to make: either retire as a teacher of kids with special needs or continue teaching for a few more years. One day while she was talking with a friend over coffee, she mentioned she was going to be a grandma for the first time. The friend shared her excitement and talked about the difficulty of having grandchildren who don't live nearby. Her friend blurted, "Cathy, you get to be a fully engaged grandma!" Although not everyone has this option, Cathy retired from her job so she could watch our grandson while his mommy went to work as a teacher herself. Their relationship is something wonderful to watch, filled with weekly trips to the library, a music class, and all the special traditions Cathy and our grandson are building together.

Build lifelong memories and traditions. I continue to collect memory-making traditions as I talk with grandparents who are doing a good job of this with their families. Here are a couple of my favorites:

- *Make Sunday family time.* Share a meal together. Gather at nearby parks or beaches and have fun. The Schroder family in Oregon opens their home to their family and friends on Sunday nights. People bring food. Kids play together. The grownups share stories or watch a game. Their weekly gathering is simple but sacred.

- *Take a vacation together.* Our family takes annual trips together. It could be something as simple as going on a weekend camping trip or renting a vacation home in the mountains, or saving up for a trip to a special place to play, rest, and spend time together. On vacations like these, leave the drama at home and just enjoy each other's company. Cathy and I share our expectations for our time together with the kids before we leave, and we always offer to watch the grandkids while their parents get some well-deserved time alone together.

- *Organize a cousins' camp.* Each year, a family we know invites all their grandkids to their house for a weekend sleepover. The grandparents plan a fun-filled time of games, experiences, and delicious food. Even as some of the grandkids are getting older, no one wants to miss out on cousins' camp.

- *Plan a special grandparents' trip.* Our friends Randy and Susan Bramel, to whom this book is dedicated, provide a most remarkable experience for each of their grandchildren at age thirteen. Each grandchild goes on a special trip alone with Grandma and Grandpa. They plan it together, and it's a once in a lifetime experience for both the grandchild and the grandparents. They have been to Cooperstown and the Baseball Hall of Fame, snorkeled with turtles in the tropics, toured Civil War battlefields, and ridden horses on a dude ranch. The destination is part of the trip, but it's much more about the lifelong memories they make together along the way.

- *Grandchild-proof your home.* Make sure there are special places reserved just for the grandkids. For my mom, it was a lower drawer in her dresser, stuffed with dress-up clothes, junk jewelry, and other fun things my daughters loved playing with. Cathy cleared out a closet that's now the grandkids' toy closet. One set of grandparents we know thought the older grandkids were getting a bit bored when they came over, so they invested in a ping-pong table and a video game console. What memories, traditions, and kid-friendly spaces might you create for your grandchildren?

Offer grace—constantly. My job as a grandparent is to praise and support, not to give advice. One grandpa I know told me his granddaughter occasionally had moments of making poor choices as a teenager. "My place in her life was to offer her grace," he said. "When my kids were younger, I was much tougher on them. Now I can allow my grandkids the opportunity to make mistakes and it doesn't matter as much to me. Offering grace is more powerful than any correction I could give them."

Celebrate everything. Be the kind of grandparent who doesn't miss an opportunity to celebrate. Birthdays, graduations, school promotions, and any kind of new markers in your grandkids' lives are opportunities to celebrate. Don't be the kind of grandparent who gives socks and underwear. Choose fun gifts and make celebrations a big deal. As you celebrate and recognize the rites of passage in your grandkids' lives, you weave a beautiful memory into your heart and theirs, a memory that you were present and cheered them on.

Recognize your role as a mentor. A mentor is an experienced and trusted advisor. You have experiences and wisdom your grandchildren might not get from anyone else. Mentoring doesn't always come from a formal relationship; it also comes from spontaneous moments of impact that can happen only when you are present in their lives. Even if you feel you didn't do your best with your kids, you get a fresh start with your grandkids. As their mentor, you can be that safe and secure place for them simply to be themselves. Your positive influence can be their hope in times of turmoil. If their world is falling apart, you can be the one they know they can come to for wisdom as well as comfort.

Keep supporting your adult children in their role as parents. I like this phrase: "Assist the parents and don't impose." It's important to remember that your job as a parent and grandparent is not to meddle but to come alongside and help. This means you don't give advice unless asked. You'll have to do it their way and let go of thinking it must be done your way, even if you are right. Your relationship with your adult children is the single most important gateway to your grandchildren. They are the gatekeepers and you are to honor that relationship. Your love for your grandchildren is a different kind of love that is not so burdened by parenting responsibilities.[29]

THE UNVEILING OF A NAME

Some memories you just never ever forget. My daughter Christy was pregnant with our first grandchild. She had already revealed the sex of the baby months before while Cathy and I were on a vacation in Hawaii. Christy created a box of baby boy items to show us on Facetime as a creative and visual way to tell us the sex of the baby. When we got off the phone, we walked to a nearby store where we bought a newborn baby boy's shirt, a football, and a book for boys.

The next reveal happened a few months later when our family was at a restaurant having breakfast together before church. Christy told us she had an announcement. She pulled out a children's book, handed it to me, and asked me to open it. There was an inscription written on the front page that said, "This book is the property of Baby James." It took a moment for it to hit me. This little boy would be named after *me*. I'm the guy in our family who tears up quickly, and for many awkward moments I couldn't say a word. Then I simply said, "I am so honored."

I was very quiet for the remainder of the breakfast. It was beginning to sink in that this new child, and other future children who would be welcomed into our lives, was going to dramatically change the nature of our family. But the more I thought about this child being named after me, the more I realized it was a dream come true. It was not just that he would have my name but also that he represented a new opportunity for both Cathy and me to invest in and transform generations to come.

Cathy and I call ourselves the transitional generation. We recognize the biblical truth that we are heirs to both the follies and the wisdom, the sins and the graces of previous generations. During the first year of our marriage, we decided to *recover from* rather than *repeat* the past generation's regrettable patterns and choices. We chose to be the transitional generation to give our kids an even stronger foundation than what we'd grown up with. Upon the birth of sweet Baby James, we wanted that transition to be carried on into yet another generation. Long after I'm gone and my distant descendants forget my name, there will be generations to come who are pointed in a better direction. Isn't that the legacy that we all want to leave?

Do you know the names of your great-great-great-great-grandparents? Most people I ask think about it for a moment and then don't have a clue. The crazy thing about that question is that those past generations do have an influence on you. You get your DNA from them, and you are who you are partly because of some of the decisions they made. Just as they had an impact on you, your influence on your grandchildren can play a significant role in their lives. This is the time to lean into the incredible God-given role you have in their lives and make that difference. Even if they don't remember your name, a future generation will be glad you did.

AFTERWORD

━•━

I had to laugh when I read the headline "Parents Win Suit
to Kick Thirty-Year-Old Deadbeat Son out of Their House."
I knew of parents who'd struggled to get their kids to move
out, but this was the first time I'd heard of anyone taking legal
action to do it. For a couple of weeks, this epic failure-to-launch
story was the subject of all the talk shows and the conversations around the watercooler at work. The more I investigated
it, the more it read like a dramatic novel.

The parents had tried their best to come alongside their son
when he had lost his job seven years before by offering rent-free
housing for a short time to help get him back on his feet. The
problem was that the son took advantage of their generosity but
didn't accept responsibility. In court, it was revealed that the
son never helped around the home or contributed financially,
and his parents even offered to pay his first and last month's
rent for him to move into an apartment. I'd call that an entitled
child! These parents finally resorted to giving him a series
of eviction notices and then, as a last resort, took their son to
court. The judge sided with the parents and evicted the son.

I can't imagine that will ever be your story, and I do have
concerns for the future of that family. This story, which made

national and even international news, never should have happened. Both the son and his parents could have prevented it. The parents needed to have offered some tough love and set some boundaries much earlier in life, and the son needed to move on and act like an adult by taking some responsibility. If we were sitting together at Starbucks talking about this somewhat bizarre situation, I'll bet we could come up with some insight for those parents that could have changed their situation. Here is what I think I would suggest for them and for every other parent of a child who is struggling to launch:

Develop a well-thought-out plan. Very few businesses succeed without following a business plan. The same is true with parenting. Having a plan and a strategy *before* issues arise keeps you from parenting by circumstance and chance. If you are married, it will also help to keep you and your spouse on the same page.

Parent in community, not on an island. We are not meant to parent in isolation. Cathy and I have invested ourselves in a community of replenishing relationships by participating in a small group at our church. For the past fifteen years, I've been part of a group with five other men. We meet every Tuesday morning, and their wisdom and feedback have molded my parenting and now grandparenting skills more than any book I have ever read. To be in authentic community means you can be vulnerably honest about your struggles, questions, and concerns. Do you have people in your life with whom you can be real on a regular basis? Do you have a supportive group of people who will cheer you on while also providing healthy accountability when necessary? If you don't, I encourage you to find them. Take the initiative to create that group if one doesn't already exist. Start by inviting others with adult children to read this book or experience the video curriculum with you. Quickly, you will find you are not alone in your experiences with your adult children.

Practice the principles in this book, but realize that life is messy. These nine principles are life-changing and I know they work. The problem is that sometimes, even when we attempt to practice them, we encounter unforeseen obstacles. That's to be expected. You're still human and so are your kids. Just because the principles aren't failsafe doesn't mean they don't work. Few things in life work perfectly, including your relationships, so give yourself grace and then keep going.

Trust that God is on your side. God wants the best for you and your family. He doesn't promise to take away all our problems, but he does promise to walk with us through the trials and stresses of life. When I am in tune with God—when I practice the disciplines of living out my Christian life—I am much more likely to hear his still, small voice. It's not an audible voice but a whisper or intuition, which always gives me the sense that God is close. We have the option to do life and parenting with or without God's help. Since he is the author and creator of life, I choose to trust him by keeping him and his principles close to me. I hope you will make that same choice.

As this journey of ours draws to a close, I wish we could share that cup of coffee together so I could hear about your experiences and learn from your insights. My hope and prayer is that this book will encourage and challenge you as you continue the journey with your adult child.

Remember that time I woke up at 2:30 a.m. to find that Cathy was lying awake and worried about one of our adult children? That still happens sometimes, though not quite as often as it once did. Just this week, I woke up in the middle of the night and looked over to find that Cathy was lying there already wide awake.

"Are you okay?" I asked.

"Yes," she said with a smile.

"Worried about the kids?" I asked.

"Nope," she said and smiled again. "Just couldn't sleep. Maybe it was the spaghetti sauce."

"I'd much rather you were awake because of a great meal than because of worries about one of the kids or grandkids," I said.

"All is good for now," Cathy said and patted my hand. "Get some sleep."

QUESTIONS FOR REFLECTION AND DISCUSSION

✦•✦

Chapter 1: You're Fired!

Principle 1: Your Role as the Parent Must Change

1. As your kids transition to adulthood, what makes it difficult for you to change your job description and role as a parent?

2. Many parents find it challenging to be caring without being enabling. Using your relationship with your children as a reference, how would you describe the difference between the two? What have you done that is caring? What, if anything, have you done that is enabling?

3. Many parents put all of their emotional, physical, and spiritual energy into their kids and find themselves depleted. How would you describe your situation in this regard? Are you investing more in your kids than you are in yourself? What, if anything, would you change to bring more of a healthy balance and self-care to your life?

4. What is your response to this quote from Judith Viorst: "Letting our children go, and letting our dreams for our children go, must be counted among our necessary losses"?

5. How would you describe the legacy you hope to leave your children?

Chapter 2: Keep Your Mouth Shut and the Welcome Mat Out

Principle 2: Unsolicited Advice Is Usually Taken as Criticism

1. Do you agree or disagree with this chapter's principle that unsolicited advice is usually taken as criticism? Share the reasons for your response.

2. If you have practiced keeping your mouth shut and the welcome mat out, what have you found most challenging about it?

3. In what ways, if any, has experience been a better teacher than advice in your life? How have you used or struggled to use this principle in relation to your adult child? What happened as a result?

4. Briefly describe a time you felt your adult child was making a poor choice. How did you respond? Looking back, would you say your response offered respect to your adult child? What, if anything, might you do differently now?

5. A healthy parent-to-child relationship moves from control in the early childhood years to mentoring and coaching in

the young adult years. Where are you in this transition—closer to control or closer to mentoring? What concerns do you have about moving from control to mentoring?

Chapter 3: Why Is It Taking My Kid So Long to Grow Up?

Principle 3: You Can't Ignore Your Child's Culture

1. What, if anything, in your adult children's culture has surprised you? How is their culture different from yours when you were their age?

2. Do you tend to agree or disagree with this generation's view that tolerance is an essential trait of a loving person? If your worldview is that there are nevertheless some absolute truths, what traits would you consider to be essential of a loving person?

3. Many parents have identified pornography and cohabitation as two of the biggest changes in today's culture. What is your experience of these "cringe factor" issues? What other cringe factor issues concern you about this generation of young adults and about your children?

4. Where are your children when it comes to the "faith factor"? How do they view the church and their faith?

5. Describe your experience of the "messy middle." What does it mean for you to hold on to a solid moral base while simultaneously loving your kids and others who have chosen a different way?

Chapter 4: How to Raise an Entitled Adult Child . . . or Not

Principle 4: They Will Never Know How Far the Town Is If You Carry Them on Your Back

1. Many experts consider this generation of young adults to be more entitled than previous generations. Do you agree with this perspective? Why or why not?

2. What boundaries have been difficult for you to negotiate with your adult child?

3. The sidebar "Nuggets of Wisdom about Setting Boundaries" lists four statements that are helpful to remember. Which of these statements do you find most helpful? Why?
    * "You earned it."
    * "You can choose the pain of self-discipline or the pain of regret."
    * You can't want it more than they want it.
    * When the pain of remaining the same is greater than the pain of changing, they will change.

4. Overall, would you say that clearly communicating expectations to your adult child is something you are comfortable doing or uncomfortable doing? Share the reasons for your response.

5. One of the principles for setting clear expectations is to begin with the goal in mind and to set deadlines for progress. How would you describe the goal for your adult child? What deadlines would you like to set?

Chapter 5: A Failure to Launch

Principle 5: Your Job Is to Move Them from Dependence to Independence

1. In what ways, if any, have your children experienced a failure to launch? What do you wish you had done differently?

2. To what degree do you relate to the description of a helicopter parent? When might you have hovered or been overprotective of your children?

3. What makes "landing the helicopter" difficult for some parents? What are ways to land the helicopter and move your adult child toward independence?

4. "Change always involves a sense of loss," wrote C. S. Lewis. What losses might you need to sustain to move your relationship with your adult child in a positive direction?

5. What came to mind when you read about celebrating rites of passage? In what ways, if any, did your family celebrate your rites of passage as you entered adulthood? What rites of passage might you celebrate in your adult child's life?

Chapter 6: When Your Grown Child Violates Your Values

Principle 6: You Can't Want It More Than They Want It

1. We tend to think that good parents have children who become responsible adults. How do you respond to the

statement that "even good parents have children who make poor choices"? When it comes to how young adult children lead their lives, do you believe that parents have a lot of influence, little influence, or somewhere in between? Share the reasons for your response.

2. How would you describe "tough love" in a positive, helpful way? Share any examples of how you have shown tough love to your child. What kept your actions from being simply mean or punishing?

3. When an adult child has violated your values and your heart is breaking, what are practical ways not to become a one-topic parent?

4. If you had a good friend whose adult child had strayed from the faith, how might you counsel them? What encouragement might you offer to give them hope? What steps might you encourage them to take?

5. Joni's story demonstrates the power of both the attitude and perspective we adopt on our hardships. How would you describe your attitude and your perspective right now on any poor choices your children have made? What might it mean for you to "take a victory" any way you can?

Chapter 7: The High Cost of Money

Principle 7: Financial Independence and Responsibility Is the Goal

1. Were you surprised that money problems ranked as the

most common concern among parents of adult children? Why or why not?

2. How would you describe your approach to teaching your children about money when they were younger? What, if anything, do you wish you had done differently? How might you mentor your adult children in healthy financial stewardship now?

3. More than 75 percent of parents help their adult children with finances at one time or another. How have you tended to make decisions about when to help and when not to help with finances? When might financial assistance promote dependence rather than independence?

4. Discussing estate plans as well as end-of-life desires can be awkward, but it is always good to do. How do you feel about having those conversations with your kids? If you haven't yet talked with them, what specifically is holding you back?

5. In what ways might you help your child understand that "the best things in life are not things"?

Chapter 8: In-Laws, Stepfamilies, and the Blend

Principle 8: Wear Beige and Keep Your Mouth Shut

1. When it comes to in-laws and stepfamilies, do you agree or disagree with the principle to "wear beige and keep your mouth shut"? Share the reasons for your response.

2. When you were younger or first married, were you ever on the receiving end of criticism from an in-law? If so, what insights might that experience provide to keep you from criticizing your in-laws now?

3. Share an illustration of how you or someone you know violated the principle of "don't make your child choose between you and their new family." What happened as a result? In what subtle or not-so-subtle ways might you have pressured your child to make this choice? How might you guard against doing this?

4. What unique relational pressures do you experience with your adult children around the holidays or on special occasions? What can you do or have you done to navigate family times well?

5. What was the best guidance for you in this chapter? Share the reasons for your response.

Chapter 9: It's Party Time with the Grandkids

Principle 9: Being a Grandparent May Be Your Greatest Legacy

1. What do you like best about being a grandparent? If you are not yet a grandparent, what do you most look forward to about being a grandparent?

2. Looking back, how would you describe the influence your grandparents had on you? Was the influence direct or indirect, positive or negative? In what ways does your expe-

rience or lack of experience of your grandparents shape the influence you hope to have in the lives of your grandchildren? What kind of a legacy would you like to leave them?

3. What family traditions do you most want to celebrate with your children and grandchildren from year to year? What do you hope they remember most about you because of these traditions?

4. In what practical ways might you support your adult children in their role as parents?

5. When you have breathed your last breath and are with God, how would you like to be remembered by your grandchildren?

NOTES

✦•✦

1. For more information about small group resources, visit *www.homeword.com*.

2. Judith Viorst, *Necessary Losses: The Loves, Illusions, Dependencies, and Impossible Expectations That All of Us Have to Give Up in Order to Grow* (New York: Fireside, 1998), 210.

3. Jim Burns, *Ten Building Blocks for a Solid Family* (Ventura, CA: Regal, 2010).

4. Jane Isay, *Walking on Eggshells: Navigating the Delicate Relationship between Adult Children and Parents* (New York: Doubleday, 2007), 87.

5. Ronald J. Greer, *Now That They Are Grown: Successfully Parenting Your Adult Children* (Nashville: Abingdon, 2012), 42.

6. Ruth Graham has spoken and written extensively about her life. For more information, visit *www.ruthgraham.com*.

7. Jeffrey Arnett, *Emerging Adulthood: The Winding Road from the Late Teens through the Twenties* (New York: Oxford Univ. Press, 2015), 8.

8. "Cohabitation in the United States," *Wikipedia*, en.wikipedia.org/wiki/Cohabitation_in_the_United_States.

9. Wendy D. Manning, "Trends in Cohabitation: Over Twenty Years of Change, 1987–2010," National Center for Family and Marriage Research, *https://www.bgsu.edu/content/dam/BGSU/college-of-arts-and-sciences/NCFMR/documents/FP/FP-13-12.pdf*.

10. Glenn Stanton, *The Ring Makes All the Difference* (Chicago: Moody, 2011), 61.
11. Stanton, *The Ring Makes All the Difference*, 47.
12. George Barna, *Gen Z: The Culture, Beliefs and Motivations Shaping the Next Generation* (Venture, CA: Barna Books, 2018), 25.
13. David Kinnaman and Gabe Lyons, *unChristian: What a New Generation Really Thinks about Christianity . . . and Why It Matters* (Grand Rapids: Baker, 2012), 26.
14. Kara Powell, Jake Mulder, and Brad Griffin, *Growing Young: Six Essential Strategies to Help Young People Discover and Love Your Church* (Grand Rapids: Baker, 2016), 43.
15. Hazelden Betty Ford Foundation, "What Is Enabling?" *https://www.hazeldenbettyford.org/articles/kala/enabling-fact-sheet.*
16. Allison Bottke, *Setting Boundaries with Your Adult Children* (Eugene, OR: Harvest House, 2008), 39.
17. John Townsend, *The Entitlement Cure: Finding Success in Doing Hard Things the Right Way* (Grand Rapids: Zondervan, 2015), 50.
18. Optimum Performance Institute, "Connection between an Enabling Parent and a Child's Failure to Launch," July 31, 2014, *https://www.optimumperformanceinstitute.com/failure-to-launch-syndrome/connection-parent-and-failure-to-launch.*
19. Henry Cloud and John Townsend, *Boundaries, Updated and Expanded Edition: When to Say Yes, How to Say No to Take Control of Your Life* (Grand Rapids: Zondervan, 2017), 68.
20. Jim Burns and Jeremy Lee, *Pass It On: Building a Legacy of Faith for Your Children through Practical and Memorable Experiences* (Colorado Springs: Cook, 2015).
21. HomeWord.com is an excellent resource for videos for you and for your adult children.
22. Jeffrey Jensen Arnett, and Joseph Schwab, "The Clark University Poll of Parents of Emerging Adults: Parents and Their Grown Kids; Harmony, Support, and (Occasional) Conflict," Clark University, September 2013, *www2.clarku.edu/*

*clark-poll-emerging-adults/pdfs/clark-university-poll-parents
-emerging-adults.pdf.*

23. Ron Blue and Judy Blue, *Money Matters for Parents and Their Kids* (Nashville: Thomas Nelson, 1988), 47.

24. Tae Kim, "Total US Household Debt Soars to Record above $13 Trillion," CNBC, February 13, 2018, *https://www.cnbc.com/2018/02/13/total-us-household-debt-soars-to-record-above-13-trillion.html.*

25. Maurie Backman, "Here's a Breakdown of the Average American's Household Debt," *The Motley Fool*, December 24, 2017, *https://www.fool.com/retirement/2017/12/24/heres-a-breakdown-of-the-average-americans-househo.aspx.*

26. Tim Kimmel and Darcy Kimmel, *Extreme Grandparenting: The Ride of Your Life!* (Carol Stream, IL: Tyndale, 2007), 66.

27. The Parent Cue app is available in the Apple store and online.

28. Kimmel and Kimmel, *Extreme Grandparenting*, 150.

29. This is not the advice I would give to any of the more than 2.7 million grandparents who are raising their grandchildren. For whatever reason, you are now in charge. Your sacrifice is so very admirable and you are still their grandparent, but your role must shift to "parent in charge" as well.

Also available

Doing Life with Your Adult Children
VIDEO SERIES

Practical and proven – perfect for great discussion and interaction

Based on Jim Burns' book, *Doing Life with Your Adult Children*

The series includes:

- 6 short downloadable videos teaching practical and insightful lessons and stimulating great discussion
- Great for small groups, couples or individuals
- One leader's guide
- One reproducible discussion guide for each video

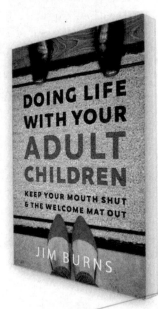

To order or get more information go to
HomeWord.com